RECORDED VERSIONS
GUITAR
AUTHENTIC TRANSCRIPTIONS
WITH NOTES AND TABLATURE

RED HOT CHILI PEPPERS
I'M WITH YOU

Music transcriptions by Pete Billmann, Addi Booth, Aurelien Budynek,
Paul Pappas, Martin Shellard and David Stocker

ISBN 978-1-4584-1726-8

HAL•LEONARD®
CORPORATION
7777 W. BLUEMOUND RD. P.O. BOX 13819 MILWAUKEE, WI 53213

In Australia Contact:
Hal Leonard Australia Pty. Ltd.
4 Lentara Court
Cheltenham, Victoria, 3192 Australia
Email: ausadmin@halleonard.com.au

Visit Hal Leonard Online at
www.halleonard.com

Monarchy of Roses

Words and Music by Anthony Kiedis, Flea, Chad Smith and Josh Klinghoffer

Verse

E5

crim - son tide ____ is flow - ing thru ____ your

*fdbk.   fdbk.

*Microphonic fdbk., not caused by string vibration.

Riff A   End Riff A

P.M. -|

Gtr. 3: w/ Riff A (7 times)

fin - gers as ____ you sleep. ____ The prom - ise of ____ a clean re - gime ____ are ____

Gtr. 1

fdbk. - - - -| fdbk. - - - - -| fdbk. - - - -|

G5   B5   Bb5

prom - is - es ____ we keep. ____ Do you like ____ it rough, ____ I ask, ____ and ____

Gtr. 2

Rhy. Fig. 1

Harm.

Gtr. 1

Rhy. Fig. 1

3

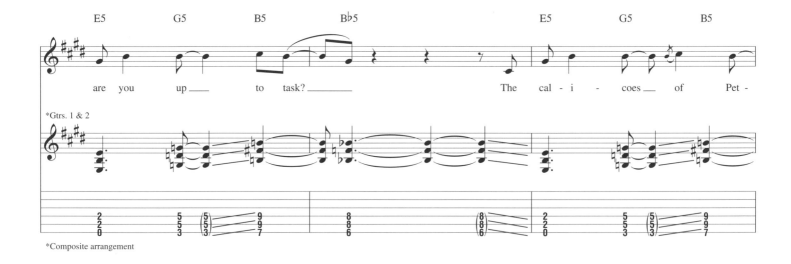

are you up __ to task? _____ The cal - i - coes __ of Pet -

*Gtrs. 1 & 2

*Composite arrangement

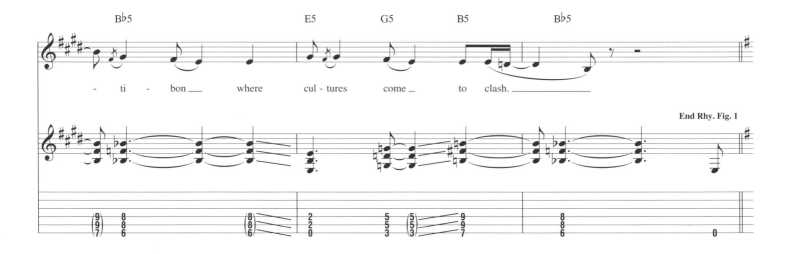

- ti - bon __ where cul - tures come __ to clash. _____

End Rhy. Fig. 1

Chorus

Gtrs. 1 & 2 tacet

Cadd9   Em

Sev - 'ral   of _____   my   best _____   friends   wear _____   the

Rhy. Fig. 2
Gtr. 4 (clean)

mf

Riff B   End Riff B
Gtr. 5 (dist.)

mp
w/ wah-wah

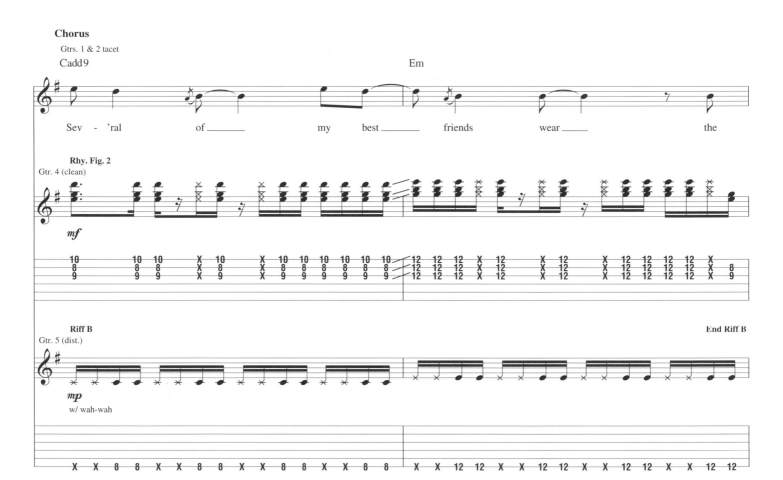

Gtr. 5: w/ Riff B (2 times)

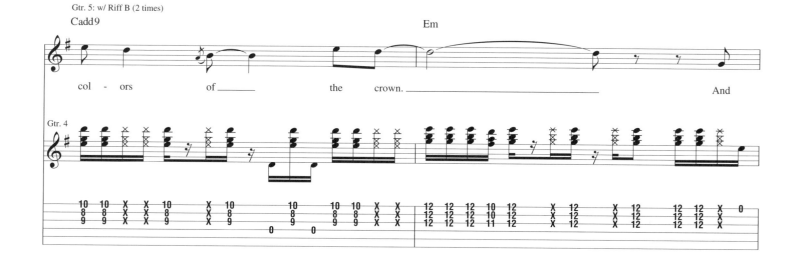

col - ors   of _____   the crown. _____   And

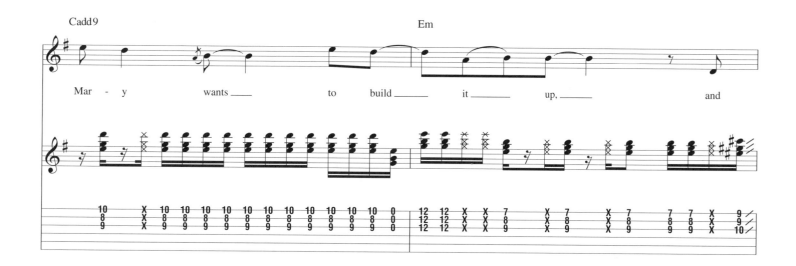

Mar - y   wants _____   to   build _____   it _____   up, _____   and

Sher - ri   wants _____   to   tear _____   it _____   all _____   back   down, ___

5

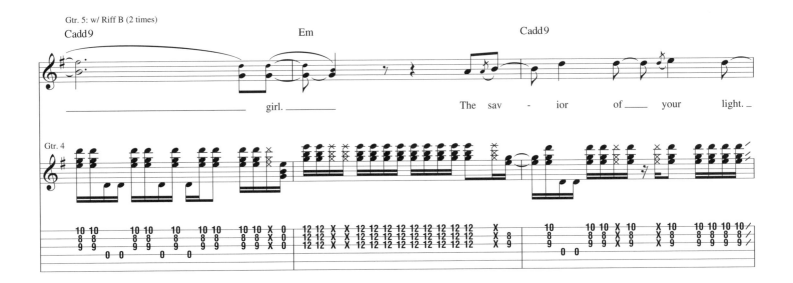

girl. _____ The sav - ior of ___ your light. __

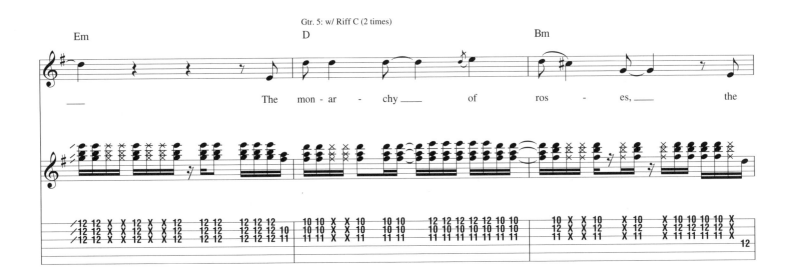

The mon - ar - chy ___ of ros - es, ___ the

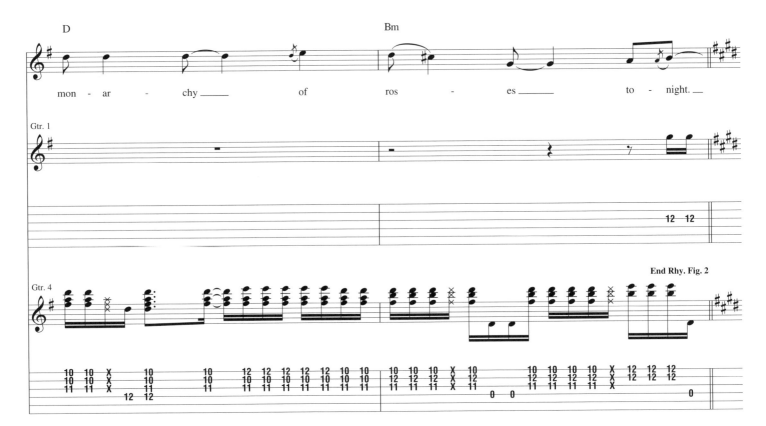

mon - ar - chy ___ of ros - es ___ to - night. __

Interlude

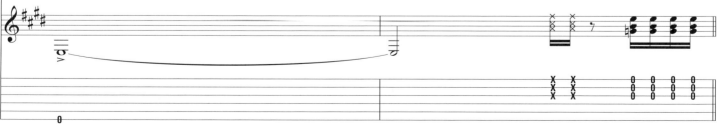

Verse

Gtr. 1: w/ Rhy. Fig. 1 (1st 6 meas.)
Gtr. 2: w/ Rhy. Fig. 1

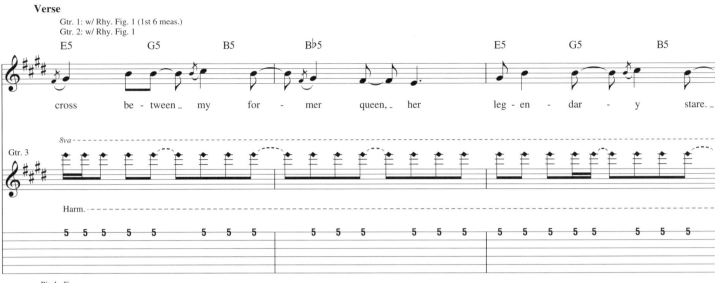

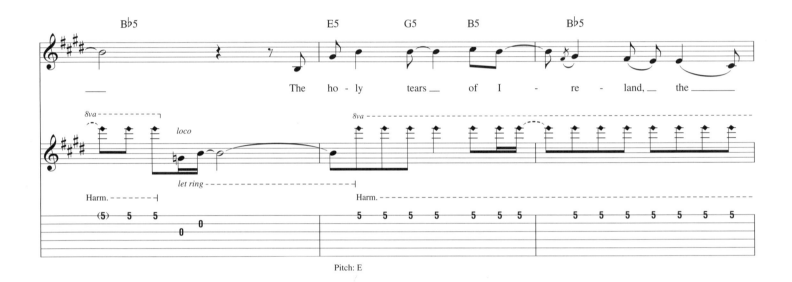

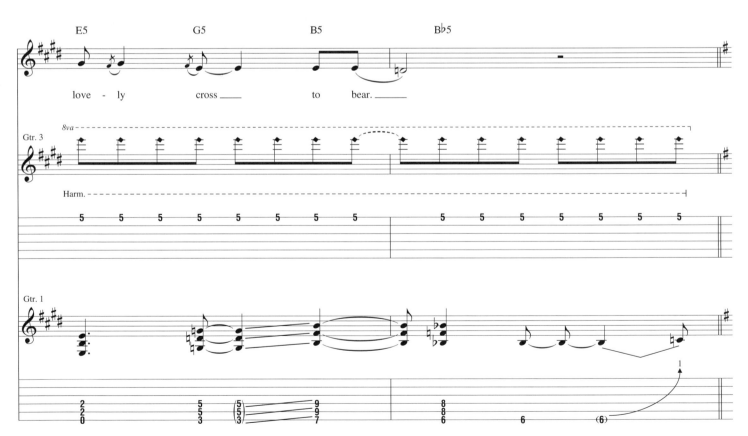

Chorus

Gtrs. 1 & 3 tacet
Gtr. 4: w/ Rhy. Fig. 2
Gtr. 5: w/ Riff B (2 times)

Sev-'ral of ___ my best ___ friends ___ know ___ the se-crets ___ of ___ this town. ___ And

Mar-y wants ___ to raise ___ it up, ___ and Sher-ri wants ___ to spin ___ it ___ all ___ a - round, ___

Gtr. 5: w/ Riff B (2 times)

___ girl. ___ The sail - ors of ___ the night. ___ The

(Ah. ___

Gtr. 5: w/ Riff C (2 times)

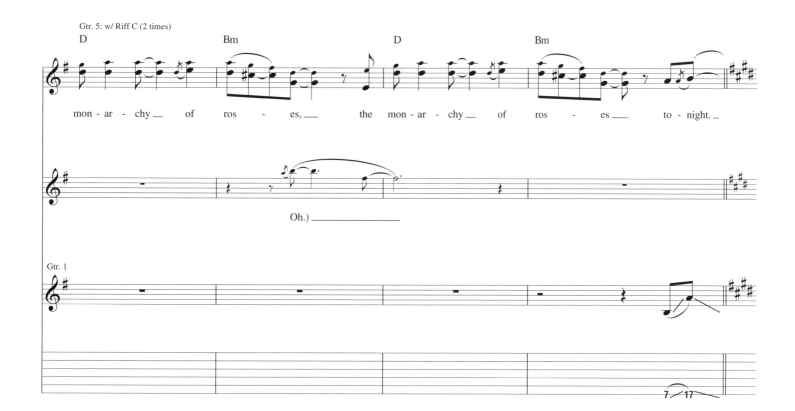

mon-ar-chy ___ of ros - es, ___ the mon-ar-chy ___ of ros - es ___ to - night. ___

Oh.) ___

Gtr. 1

9

Interlude

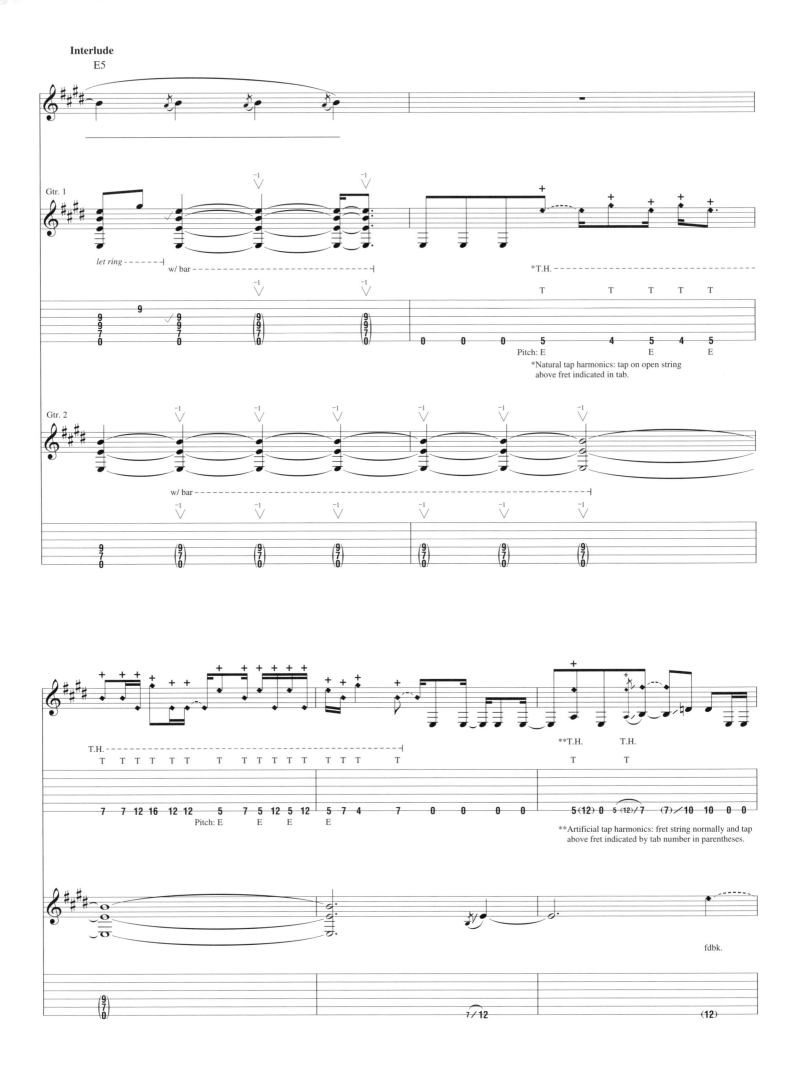

*Natural tap harmonics: tap on open string above fret indicated in tab.

**Artificial tap harmonics: fret string normally and tap above fret indicated by tab number in parentheses.

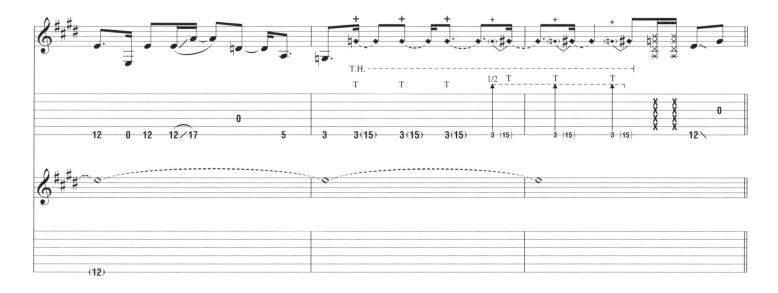

Guitar Solo

E5

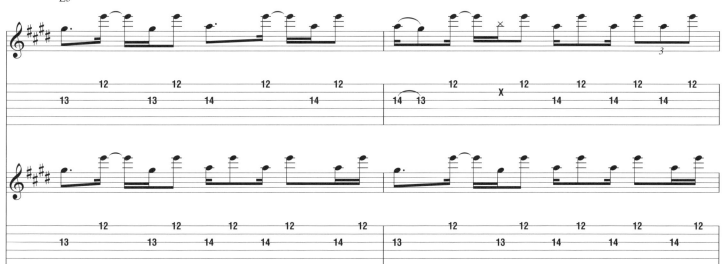

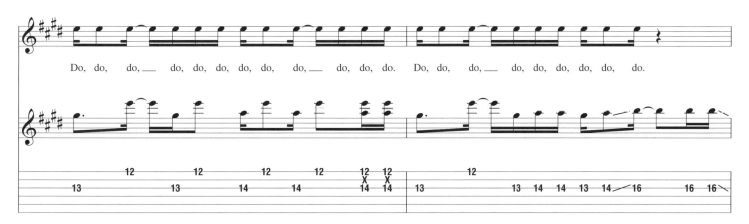

*Gtrs. 1 & 2

*Composite arrangement

Do, do, do,____ do, do, do, do, do, do,____ do, do, do. Do, do, do,____ do, do, do, do, do, do.

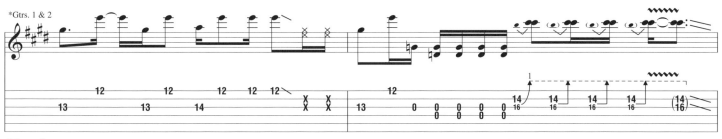

Chorus

Gtr. 4: w/ Rhy. Fig. 2
Gtr. 5: w/ Riff B (3 times)

Gtrs. 1 & 2 tacet

Sev-'ral of my best friends wear the col-ors of the crown. And

Mar-y wants to build it up, and Sher-ri wants to tear it all back down,

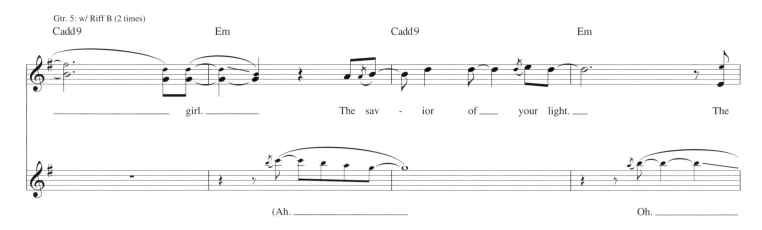

girl. The sav-ior of your light. The

(Ah. Oh.

Gtr. 5: w/ Riff C (2 times)

mon - ar - chy __ of ros - es, __ the mon - ar - chy __ of ros - es. __

__ (Oh.) _____

Gtr. 1

Bridge

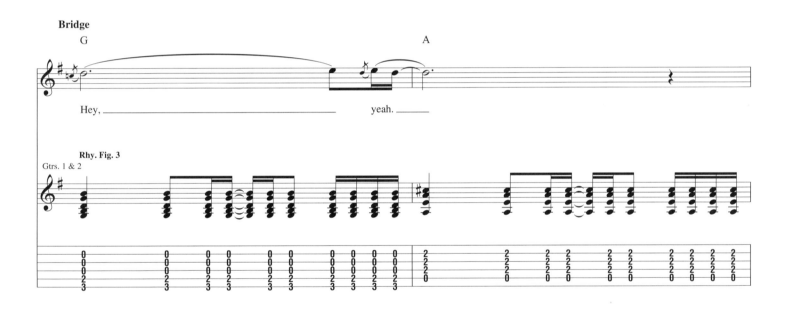

Hey, _____ yeah. _____

Rhy. Fig. 3
Gtrs. 1 & 2

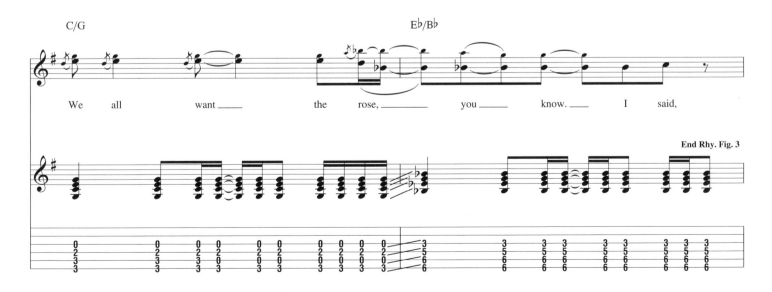

We all want ____ the rose, ____ you ____ know. ____ I said,

End Rhy. Fig. 3

14

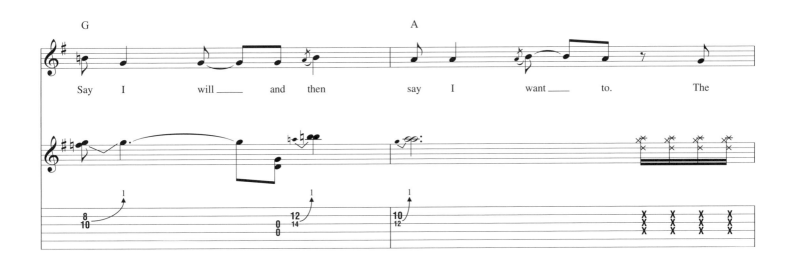

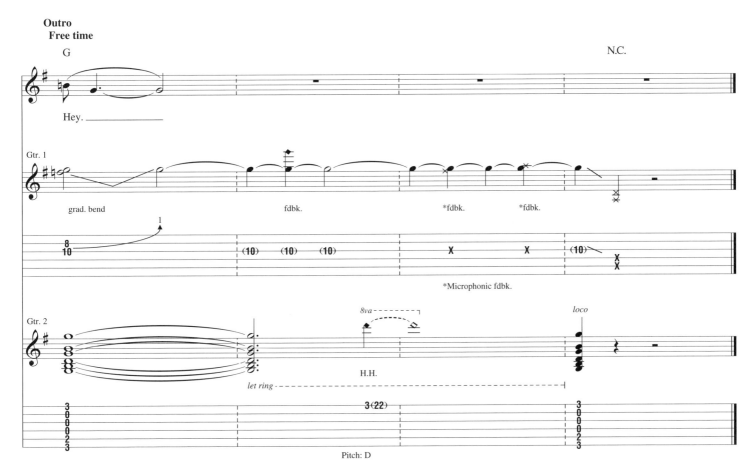

Factory of Faith

Words and Music by Anthony Kiedis, Flea, Chad Smith and Josh Klinghoffer

*Chord symbols reflect harmony implied by bass.

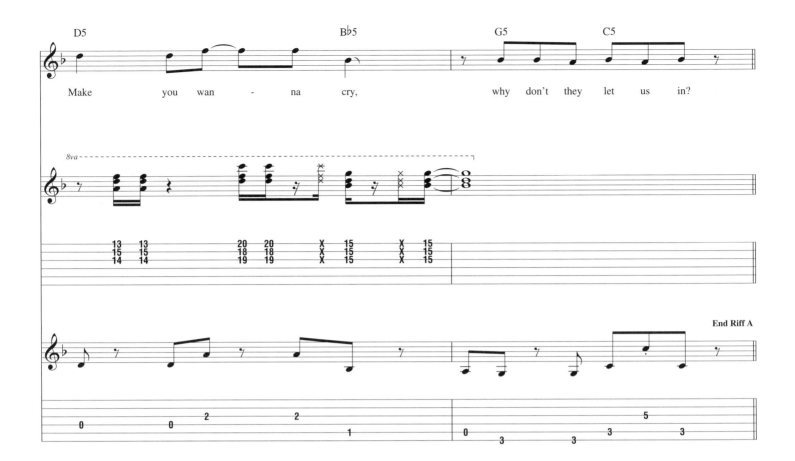

Make you wan - na cry, why don't they let us in?

End Riff A

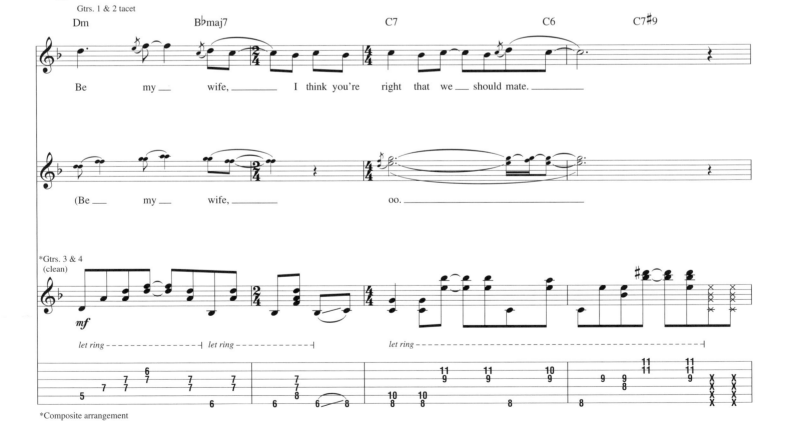

𝄋 **Chorus**

Gtrs. 1 & 2 tacet

Be my ___ wife, ___ I think you're right that we ___ should mate. ___

(Be ___ my ___ wife, ___ oo. ___

*Gtrs. 3 & 4
(clean)

mf

let ring - - - - - - - - - - - -   let ring - - - - - - - - - - - - -   let ring - - - - - - - - - - - -

*Composite arrangement

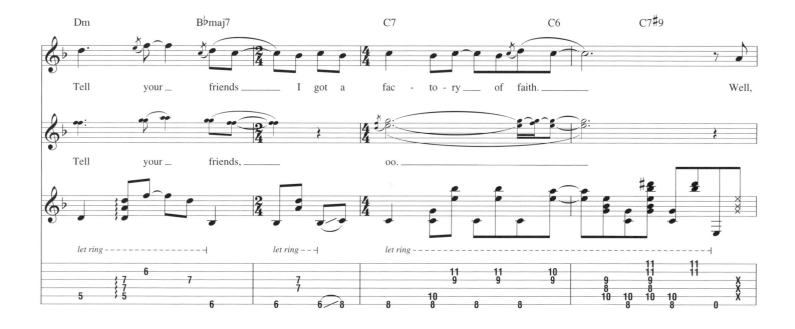

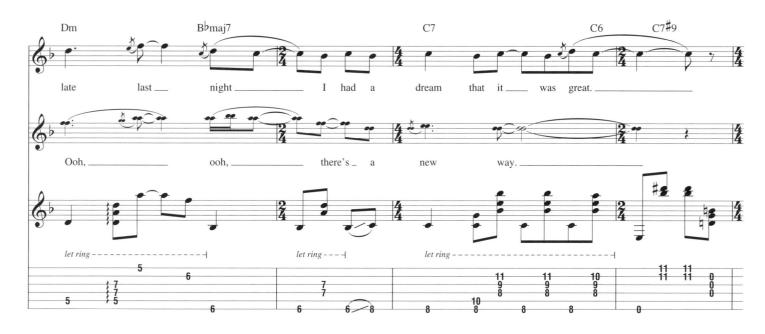

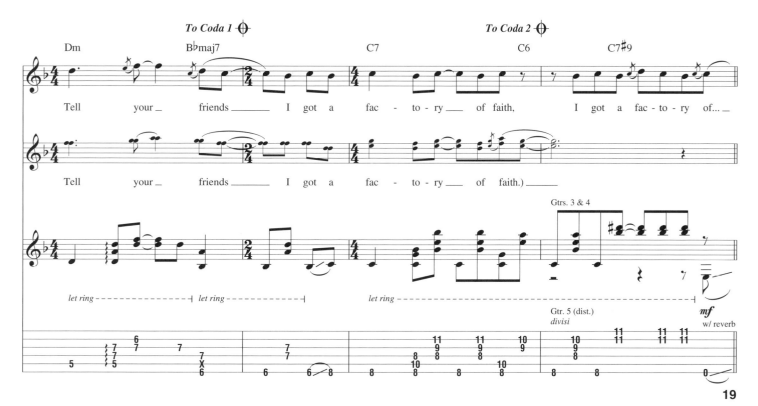

19

Interlude

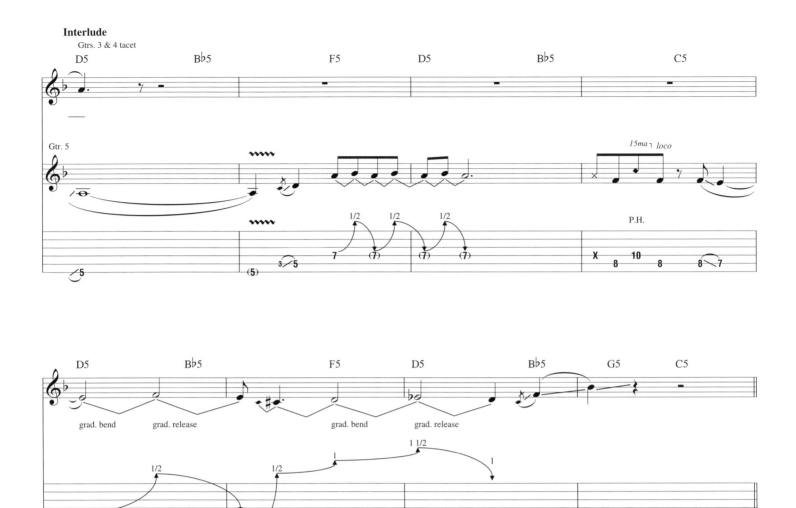

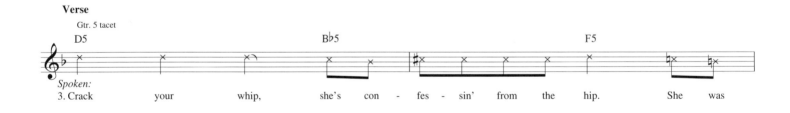

Verse

Spoken:
3. Crack your whip, she's con - fes - sin' from the hip. She was

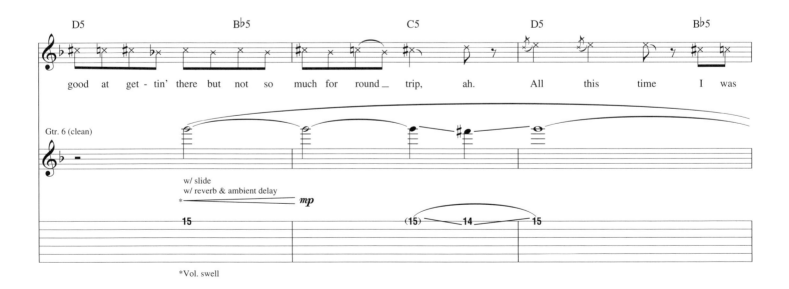

good at get - tin' there but not so much for round __ trip, ah. All this time I was

*Vol. swell

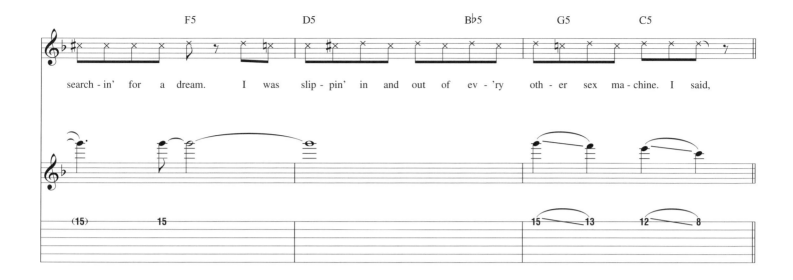

search-in' for a dream. I was slip-pin' in and out of ev-'ry oth-er sex ma-chine. I said,

Pre-Chorus

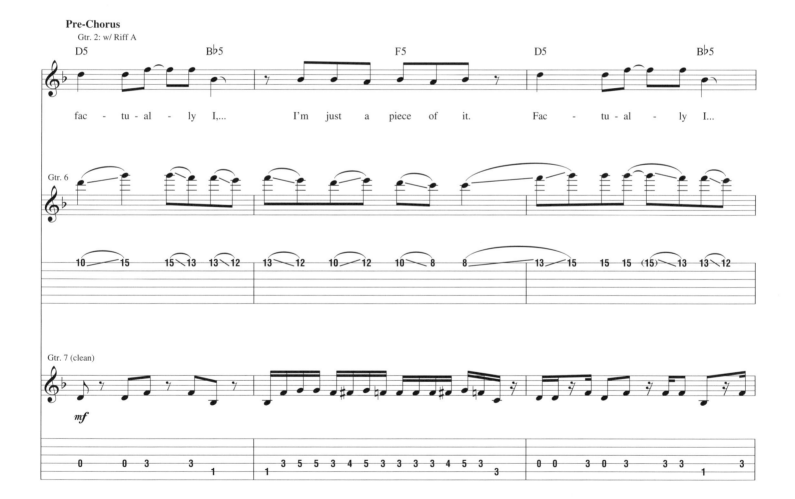

fac-tu-al-ly I,... I'm just a piece of it. Fac-tu-al-ly I...

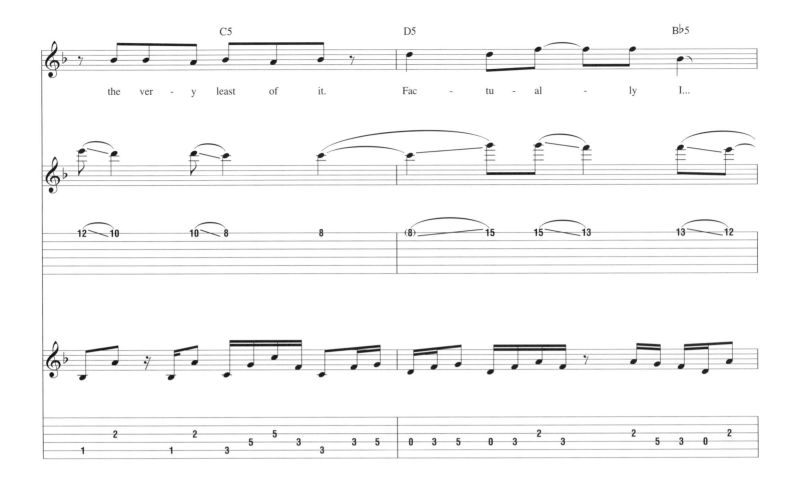

the ver - y least of it. Fac - tu - al - ly I...

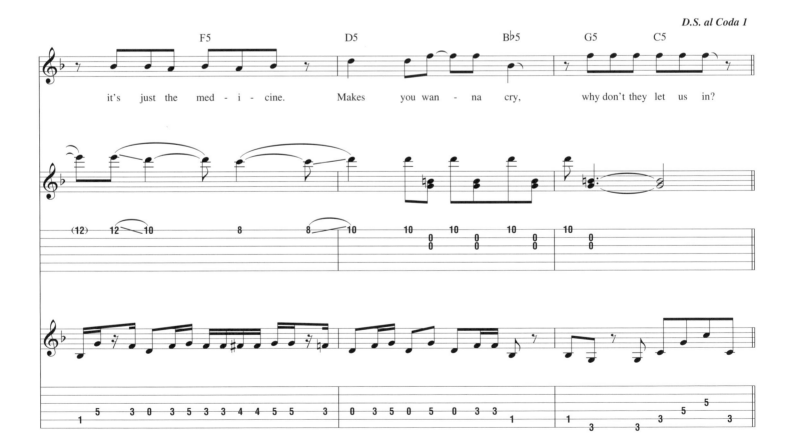

it's just the med - i - cine. Makes you wan - na cry, why don't they let us in?

Coda 1

I got a fac-to-ry of faith. I got a fac-to-ry of...

oo.

(Fac - to - ry of faith.)

ah.)

let ring

let ring

Interlude

Gtr. 3 tacet

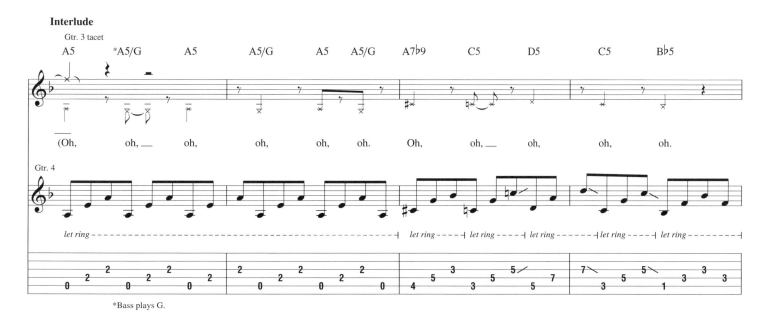

(Oh, oh, oh, oh, oh, oh. Oh, oh, oh, oh, oh.

Gtr. 4

let ring

*Bass plays G.

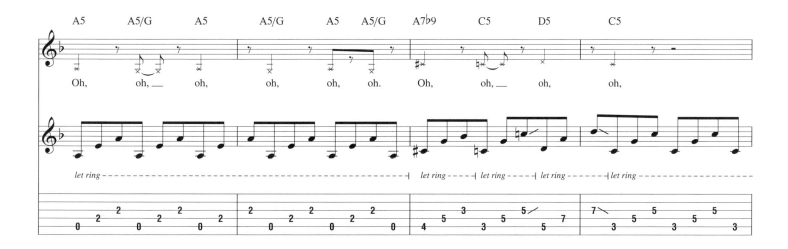

Oh, oh, oh, oh, oh, oh. Oh, oh, oh, oh,

let ring

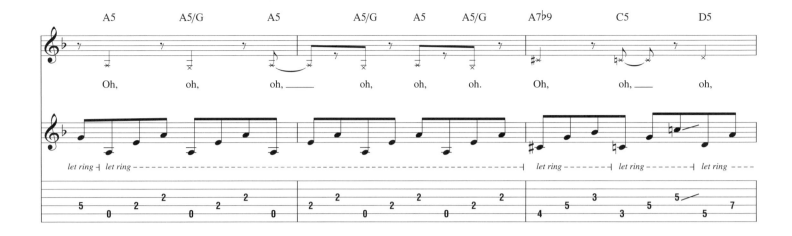

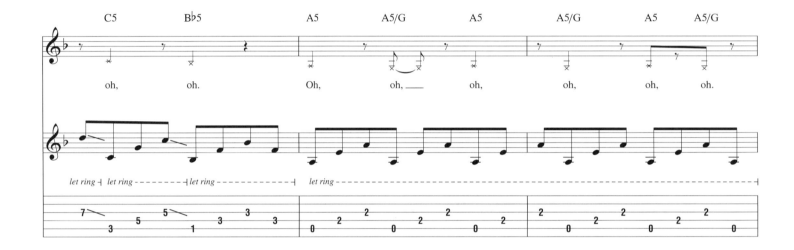

D.S. al Coda 2

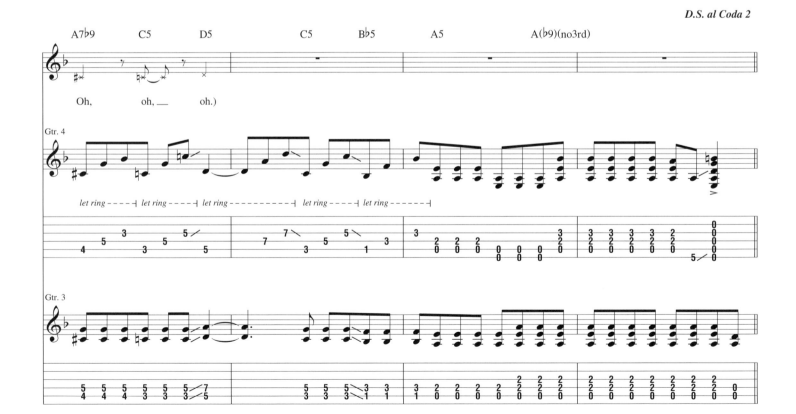

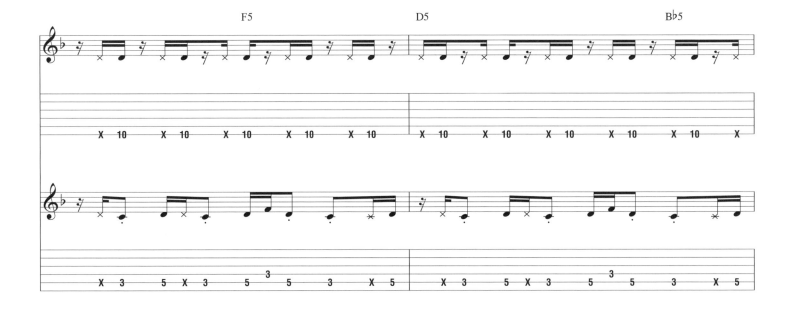

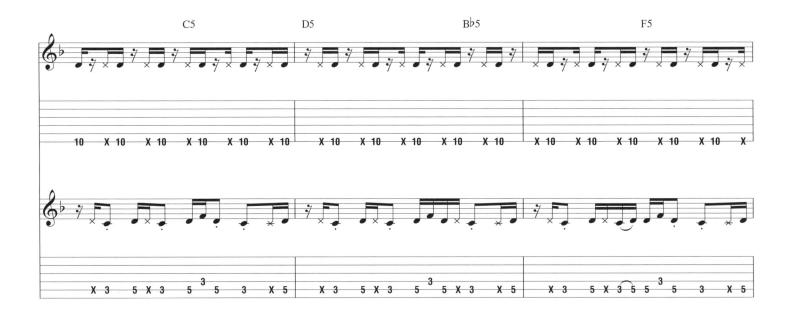

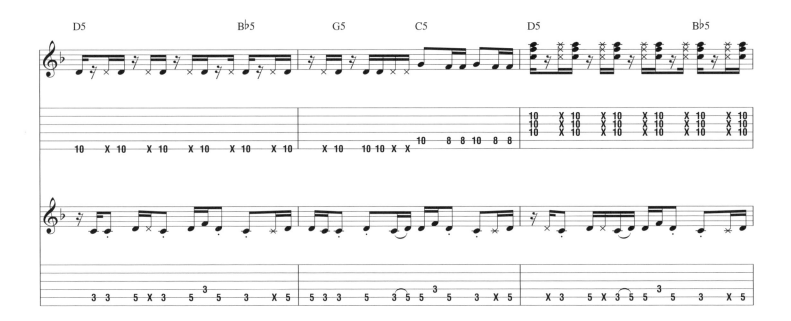

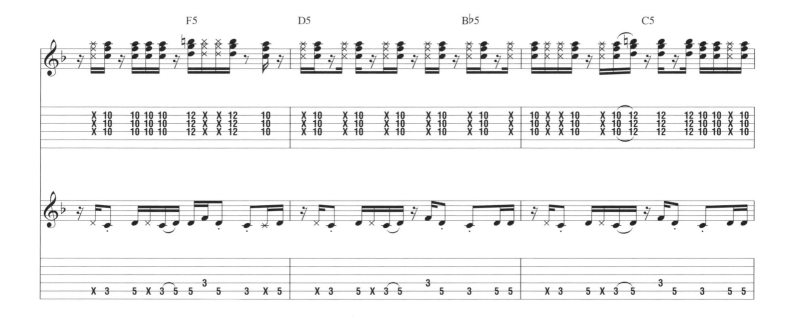

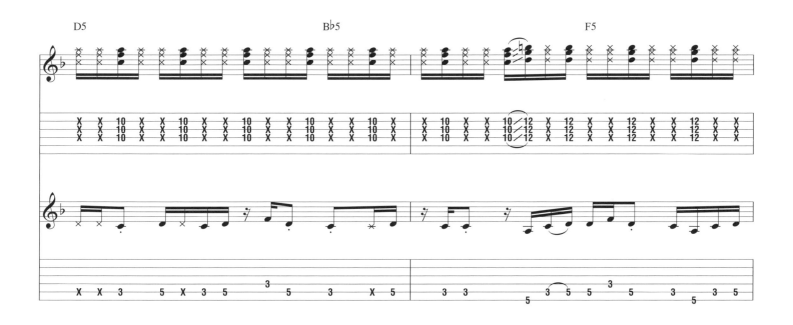

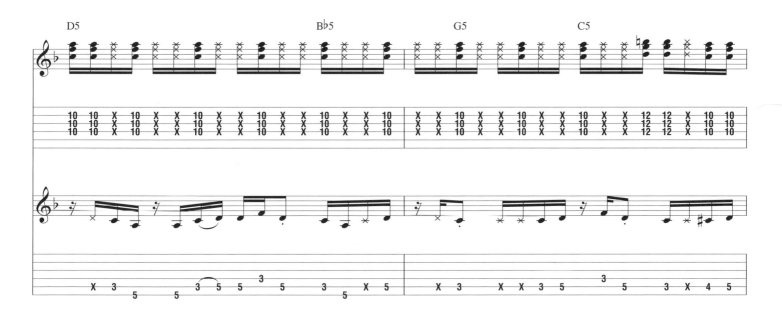

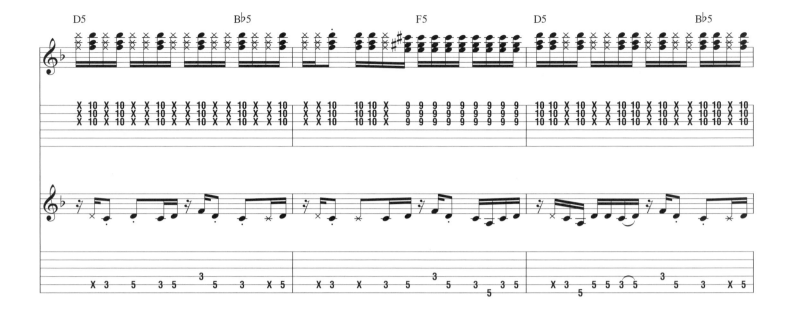

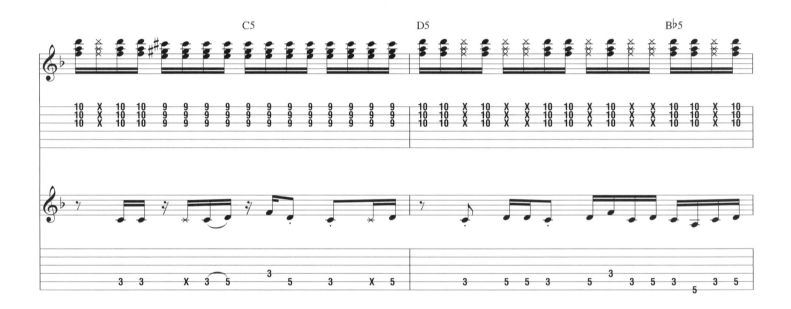

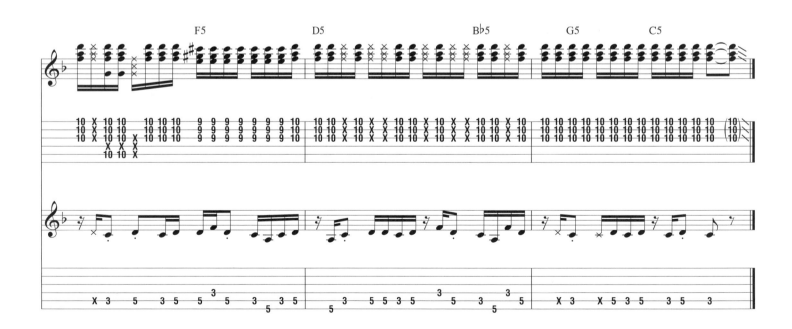

Brendan's Death Song

Words and Music by Anthony Kiedis, Flea, Chad Smith and Josh Klinghoffer

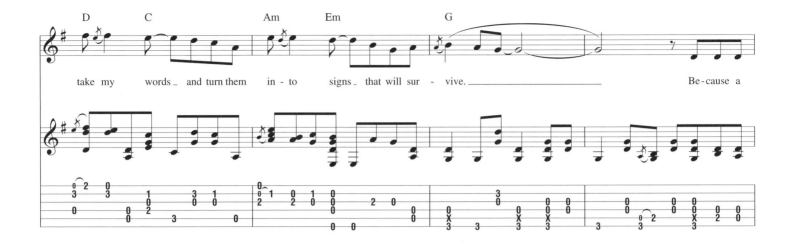

take my words___ and turn them in-to signs___ that will sur - vive.___ Be-cause a

long time___ a-go I knew___ not to de - prive.___ 2. It's

End Rhy. Fig. 1

Verse

Gtr. 1: w/ Rhy. Fig. 1

safe out there___ and now you're ev-'ry - where___ just like the sky.___

Rhy. Fig. 2

Gtr. 2 (elec.)

mf

w/ clean tone

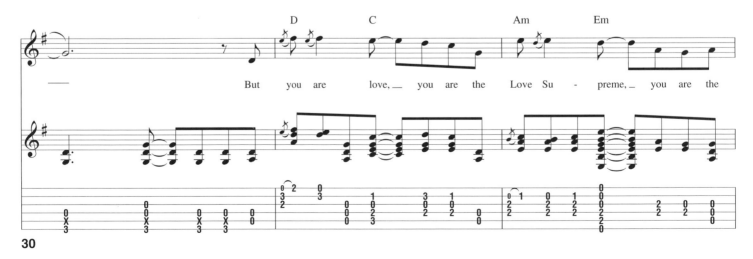

But you are love,___ you are the Love Su - preme,___ you are the

rise. _____ And when you hear this ___ you know it's

your jam, ___ it's your good - bye. _____

End Rhy. Fig. 2

Chorus

*G5   C   Em   G5

Gtr. 3
(elec.)
mf
w/ slight dist.

*string
noise*

Like I said, ___ you know I'm al-most dead, you know I'm al-most gone. _____ And when the

Voc. Fig. 1

(Oo,

Gtr. 2

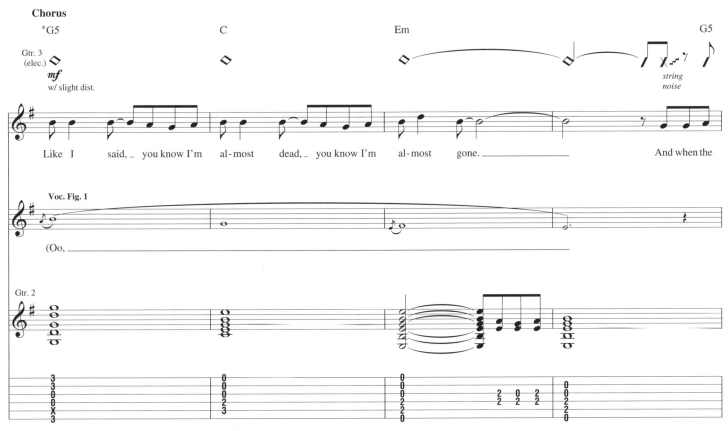

*See top of first page of song for chord diagrams pertaining to rhythm slashes.

Gtrs. 2 & 3: w/ Rhy. Figs. 3 & 3A

boat-man comes to fer-ry me a-way to where we all be-long...

Gtr. 4

Verse

Gtr. 1: w/ Rhy. Fig. 1
Gtr. 2: w/ Rhy. Fig. 2

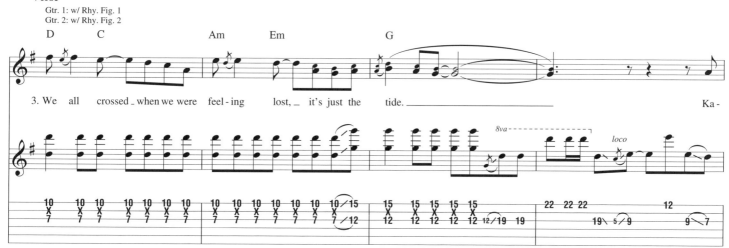

3. We all crossed when we were feel-ing lost, it's just the tide. Ka-

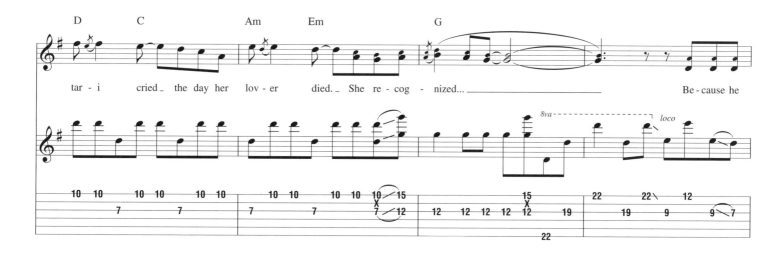

tar-i cried the day her lov-er died. She re-cog-nized... Be-cause he

gave her a life of real love, it's no sur-prise. 4. The

33

Verse

Gtr. 1: w/ Rhy. Fig. 1
Gtr. 2: w/ Rhy. Fig. 2

nights are long _____ but the years are short __ when you're a - live. _____

Voc. Fig. 2   End Voc. Fig. 2

(Oh.) _____

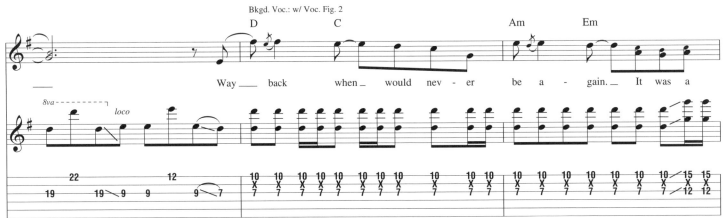

Bkgd. Voc.: w/ Voc. Fig. 2

Way ___ back when __ would nev - er be a - gain. It was a

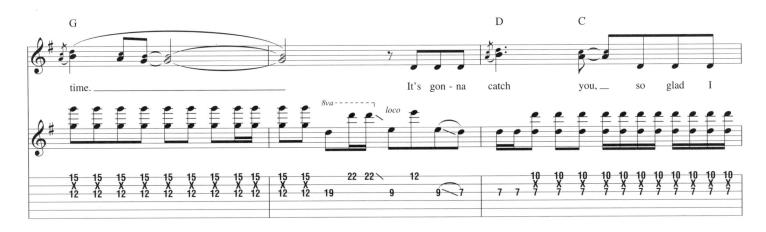

time. _____ It's gon - na catch you, __ so glad I

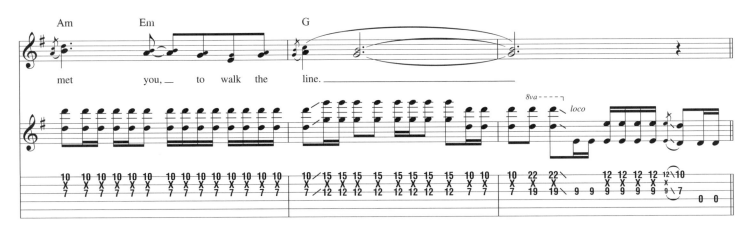

met you, __ to walk the line. _____

Chorus

Bkgd. Voc.: w/ Voc. Fig. 1 (2 times)
Gtrs. 2 & 3: w/ Rhy. Figs. 3 & 3A (4 times)
Gtr. 4 tacet

Like I said, _ you know I'm al-most dead, _ you know I'm al-most gone. ___ And when the

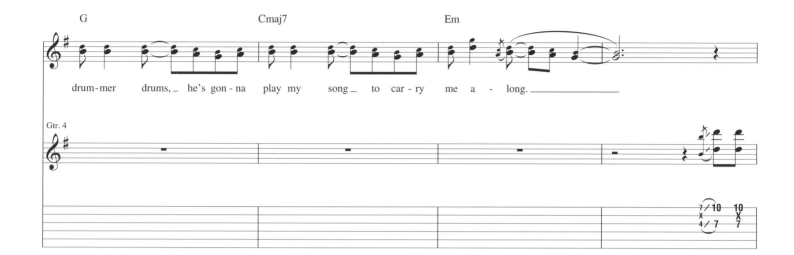

drum-mer drums, _ he's gon-na play my song _ to car-ry me a - long. ___

Gtr. 4

Like I said, _ you know I'm al-most dead, _ you know I'm al-most gone. ___ And when the

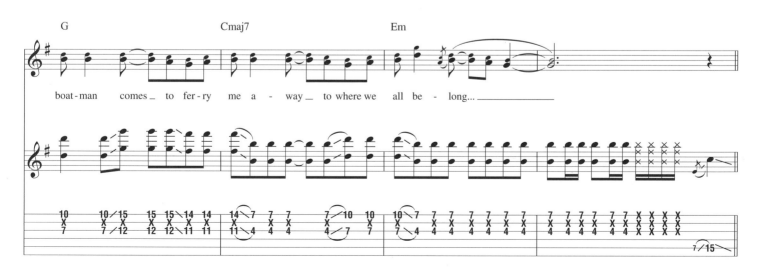

boat-man comes _ to fer-ry me a - way _ to where we all be - long... ___

35

Interlude

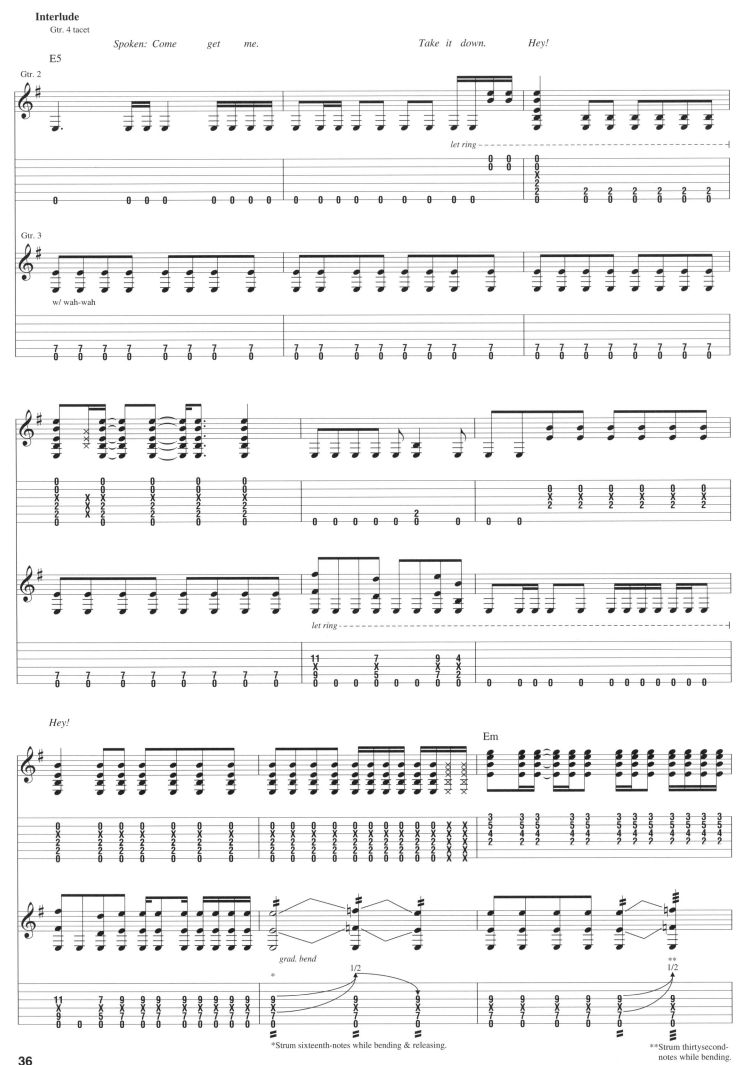

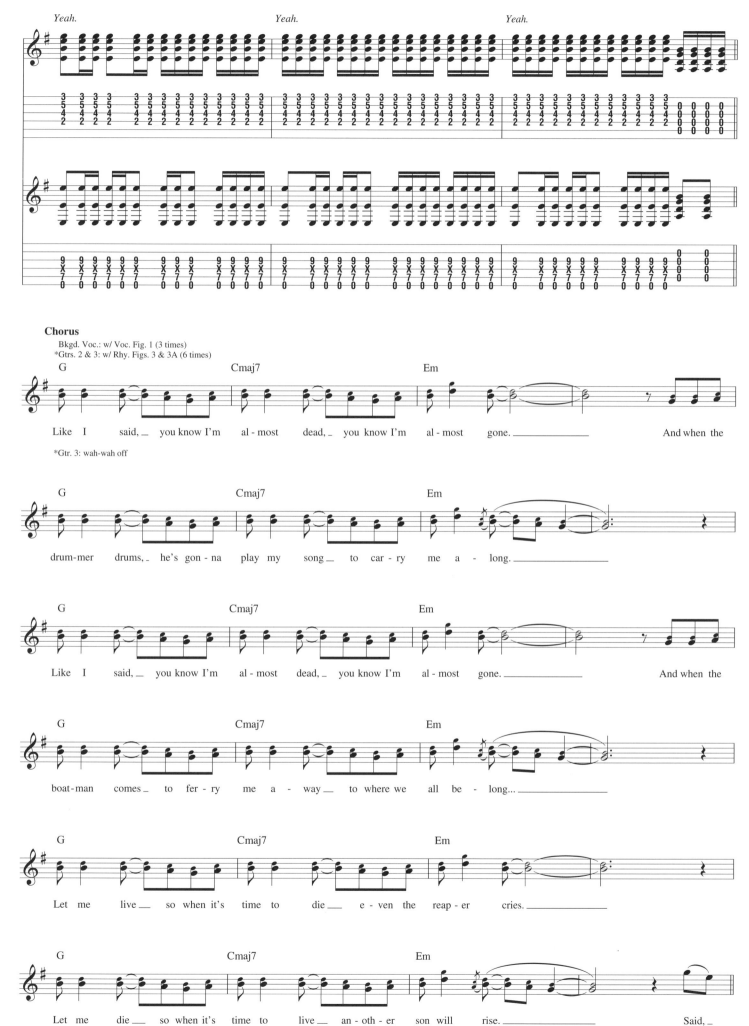

Chorus

Bkgd. Voc.: w/ Voc. Fig. 1 (3 times)
*Gtrs. 2 & 3: w/ Rhy. Figs. 3 & 3A (6 times)

G · Cmaj7 · Em

Like I said, __ you know I'm al - most dead, __ you know I'm al - most gone. _____ And when the

*Gtr. 3: wah-wah off

G · Cmaj7 · Em

drum - mer drums, __ he's gon - na play my song __ to car - ry me a - long. _____

G · Cmaj7 · Em

Like I said, __ you know I'm al - most dead, __ you know I'm al - most gone. _____ And when the

G · Cmaj7 · Em

boat - man comes __ to fer - ry me a - way __ to where we all be - long... _____

G · Cmaj7 · Em

Let me live __ so when it's time to die __ e - ven the reap - er cries.

G · Cmaj7 · Em

Let me die __ so when it's time to live __ an - oth - er son will rise. _____ Said, __

Interlude

Gtr. 2: w/ Rhy. Fig. 3 (2 times)

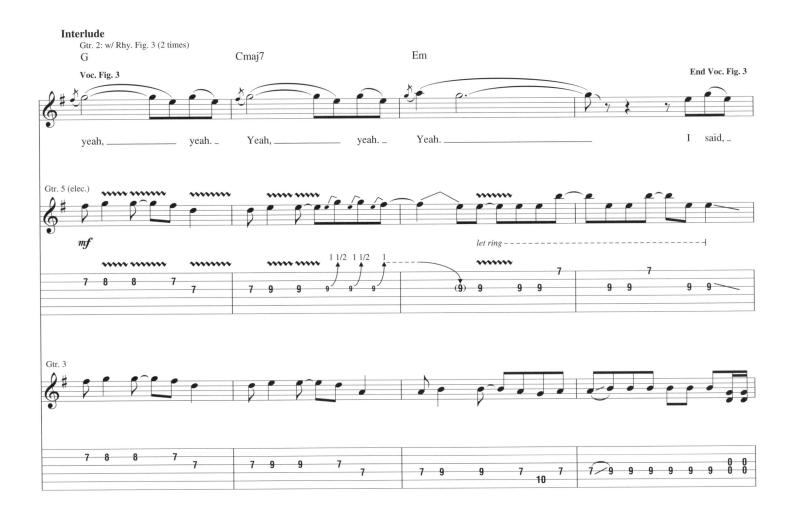

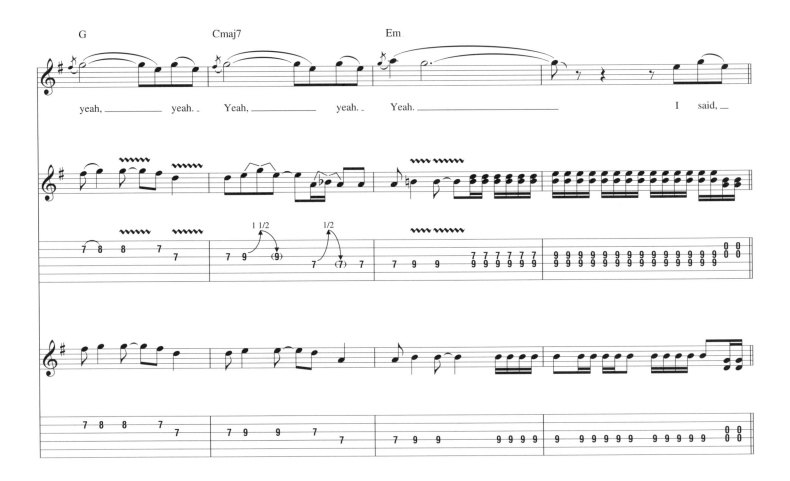

Chorus

*Bkgd. Voc.: w/ Voc. Fig. 3 (4 times)
Gtr. 2: w/ Rhy. Fig. 3 (4 times)
Gtr. 5 tacet

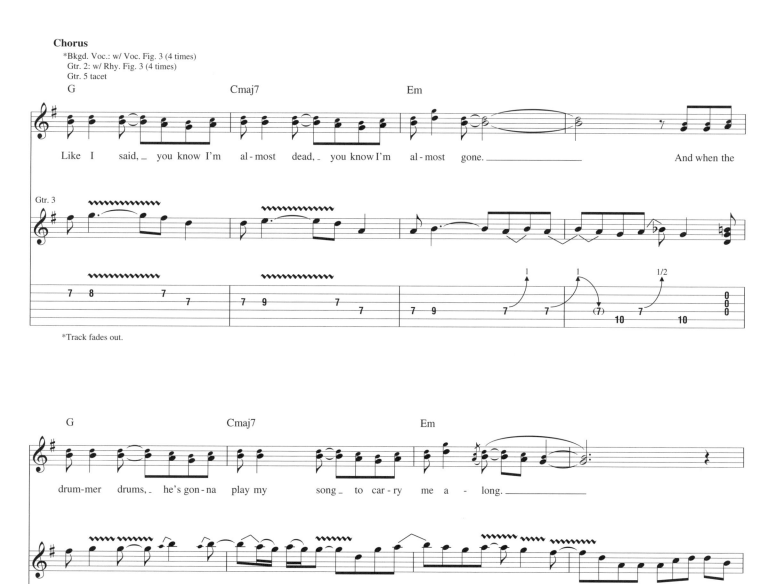

Like I said, _ you know I'm al-most dead, _ you know I'm al-most gone. _____ And when the

*Track fades out.

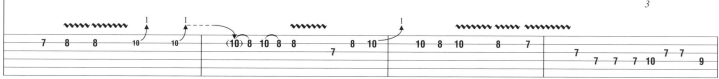

drum-mer drums, _ he's gon-na play my song _ to car-ry me a - long. _____

Bkgd. Voc.: w/ Voc. Fig. 1

Like I said, ____ you know I'm al-most dead, ____ you know I'm al-most gone. _____

And when the boat-man comes_ to fer-ry me a - way_ to where we

all be - long... _____

(cont. in notation)

*Like I said,_ you know I'm al-most dead,_ you know I'm al-most gone. _____

Gtr. 3

rit. poco a poco

rit. poco a poco

grad. bend

*Gtrs. 1 & 2

rit. poco a poco

let ring - - - - - - - - - - - - - - -

*Composite arrangement

Like I said, __ you know I'm al-most dead, __ you know I'm al-most gone. _____

(Like I said.) _____

Like I said, __ you know I'm al-most dead, __ you know I'm al-most gone.

let ring - - - - - - - - - - - - - - - - | *let ring* - - - - - - - - - - - - - - - | *let ring* - - - - - - - - - - - - - - - - |

Ethiopia

Words and Music by Anthony Kiedis, Flea, Chad Smith and Josh Klinghoffer

Gtr. 2: w/ Riff B

More and more I wan-na raise, raise my bar and raise your stakes.

E I O I E I A. When I lie there wide a-wake for my son I'll make. Tell

Gtr. 2

Fill 1   End Fill 1

let ring   *let ring*

Gtr. 3 (slight dist.)

Rhy. Fill 1   End Rhy. Fill 1

% **Chorus**

my boy I love him so. Tell him so he knows.

Rhy. Fig. 1
Gtrs. 2 & 3

let ring   *let ring*

**Composite arrangement

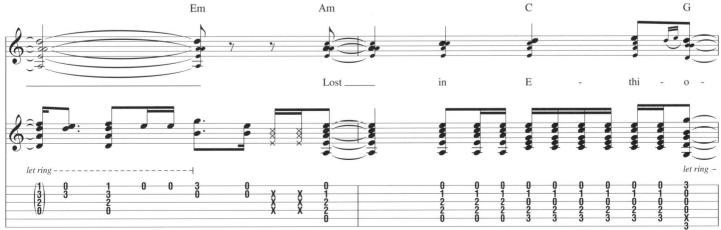

Lost in E - thi - o -

let ring   *let ring*

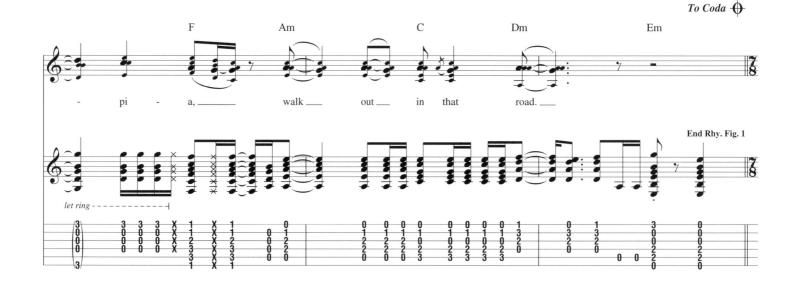

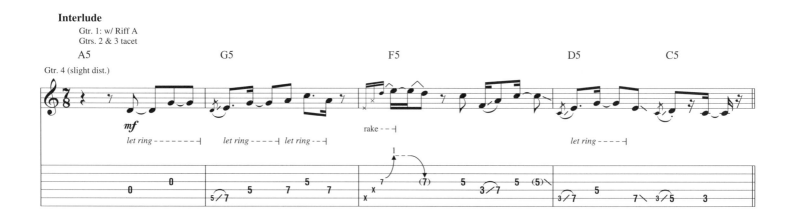

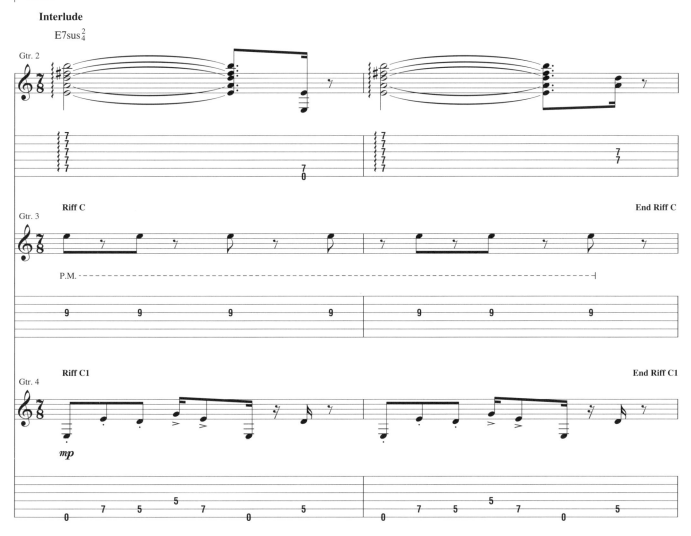

Interlude

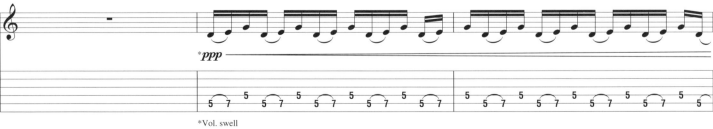

Verse

Gtr. 1: w/ Riff A (1 3/4 times)
Gtr. 3 tacet

3. E I O I E I A.   Steal my heart to give ___ a - way.   Make me ___ want to say ___

Gtr. 2: w/ Riff B (1st 3 meas.)

Gtr. 2: w/ Fill 1
Gtr. 3: w/ Rhy. Fill 1

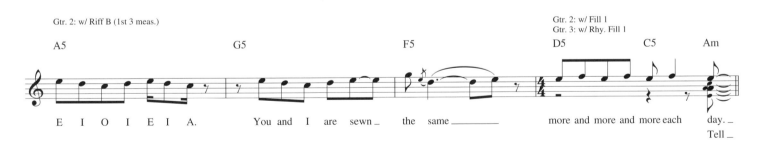

E I O I E I A.   You and I are sewn ___ the same _____   more and more and more each day. ___
                                                                                                      Tell ___

Chorus

Gtrs. 2 & 3: w/ Rhy. Fig. 1

___ my boy I love ___ him so.   Tell ___ him so he knows. _____   Lost ___

in E - thi - o - pi - a, _____ walk ___ out __ in that road. ___

Outro

48

Annie Wants a Baby

Words and Music by Anthony Kiedis, Flea, Chad Smith and Josh Klinghoffer

Verse

Gtr. 1: w/ Riff A (4 times)

2. Drink-in' sun - shine, she likes the taste of it. She had a gold - mine but then she was - ted it a -

way. _____ You should - a seen her yes - ter - day. _____ Oh, yeah. _____

Pre-Chorus

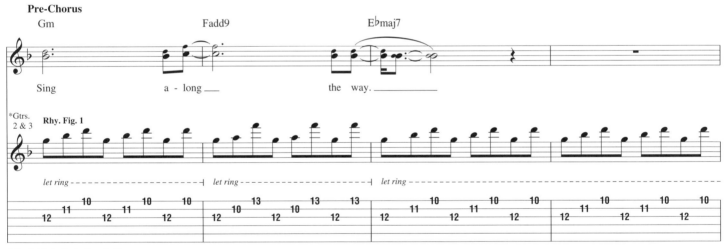

Sing a - long _____ the way. _____

*Gtr. 3 (slight dist.), played *mf*

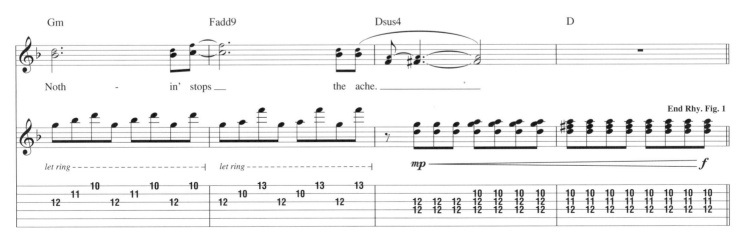

Noth - in' stops _____ the ache. _____

Chorus

Su - gar _____ dad - dy, _____ uh, loves her _____ mad _____ ly.

*Bass plays B♭.   **Bass plays D♭.   ***Bass plays C.

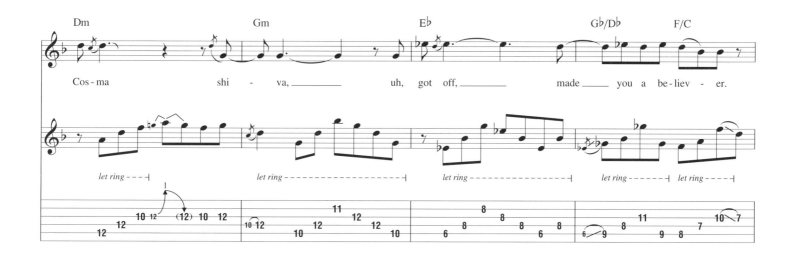

Cos - ma _____ shi - va, _____ uh, got off, _____ made _____ you a be - liev - er.

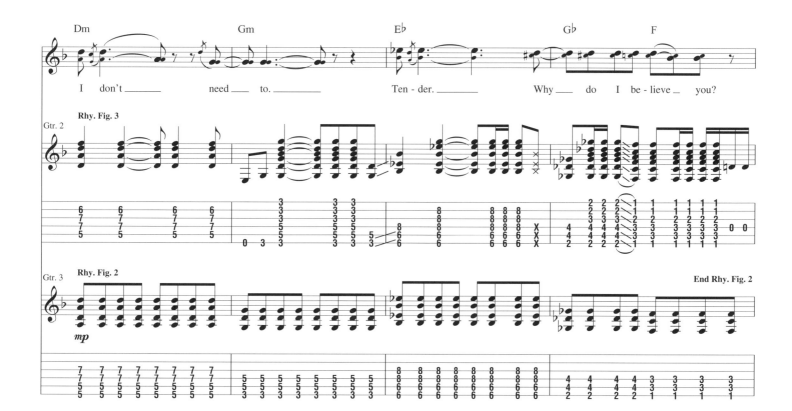

I don't _____ need __ to. _____ Ten - der. _____ Why ___ do I be - lieve __ you?

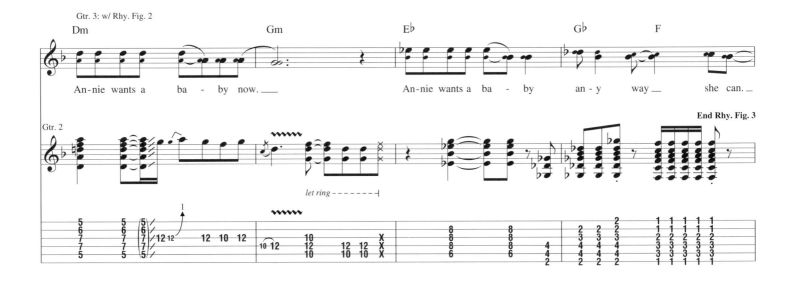

An-nie wants a ba - by now.＿ An-nie wants a ba - by an - y way ＿ she can.＿

Interlude

*Set for eighth-note regeneration w/ 4 repeats.

Verse

Gtr. 1: w/ Riff A (3 1/2 times)
Gtr. 2: w/ Riff B (1st 2 meas.)
Gtrs. 3 & 4 tacet

3. Mis - sin' piec - es, she's got a lot of 'em.

Time de - creas - es. I wish I thought of 'em be - fore,____

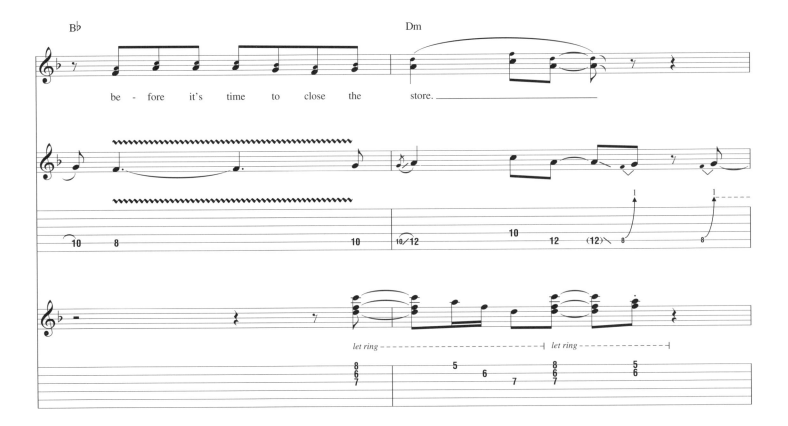

be - fore it's time to close the store. _____

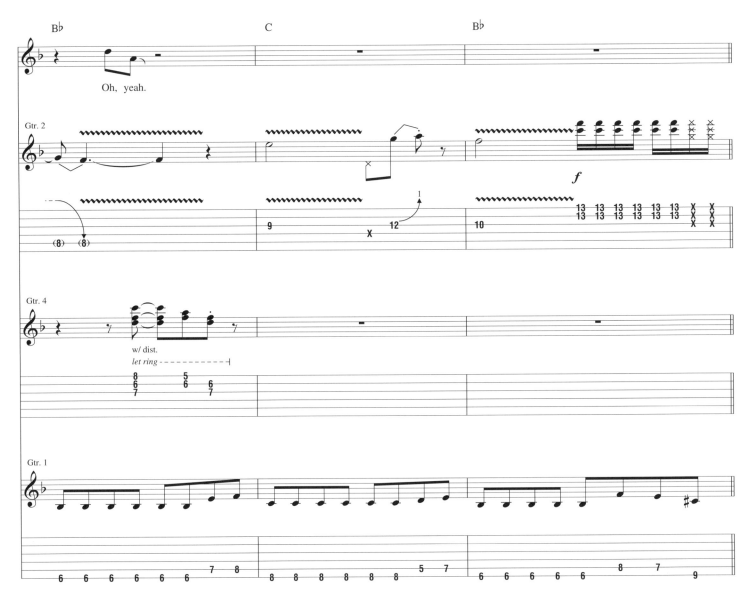

Oh, yeah.

Verse

Gtr. 1: w/ Riff A (4 times)

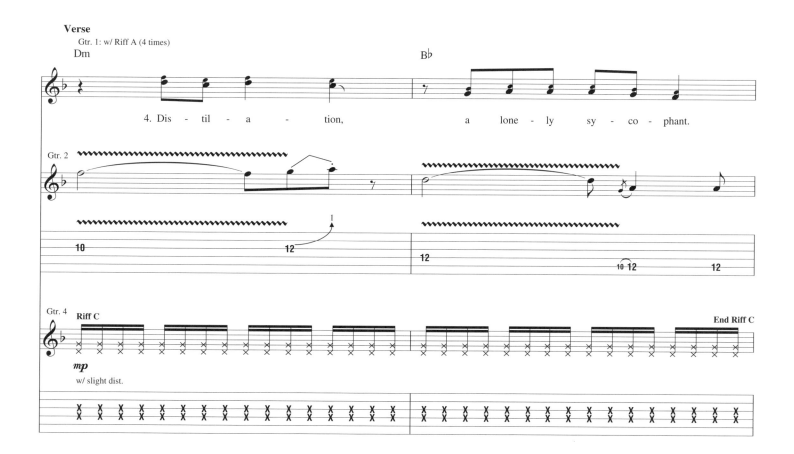

4. Dis - til - a - tion, a lone - ly sy - co - phant.

Gtr. 4 **Riff C**

mp

w/ slight dist.

End Riff C

Gtr. 4: w/ Riff C (3 times)

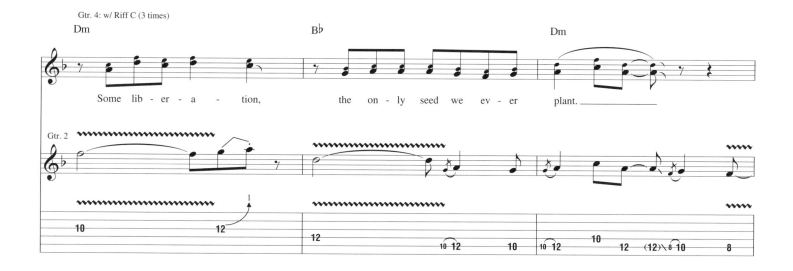

Some lib - er - a - tion, the on - ly seed we ev - er plant.

Gtr. 2

I wan - na help you but I can't. No, no.

Pre-Chorus

Gtrs. 2 & 3: w/ Rhy. Fig. 1

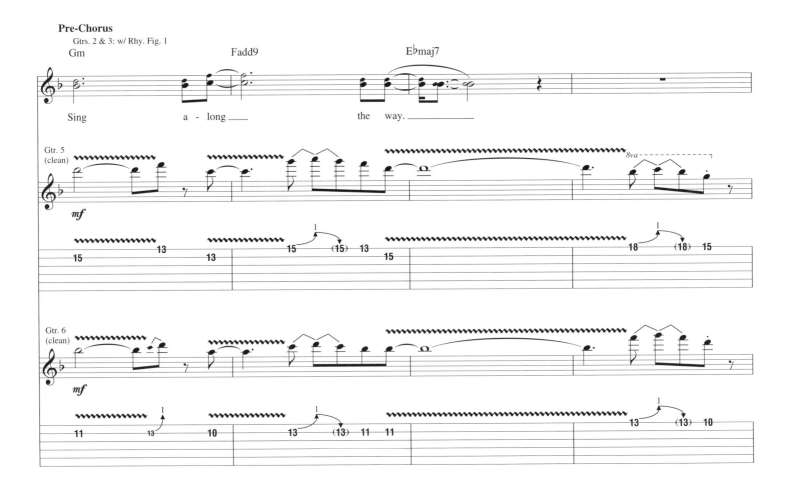

Sing a - long ___ the way. ___

Gtr. 5 (clean)

mf

Gtr. 6 (clean)

mf

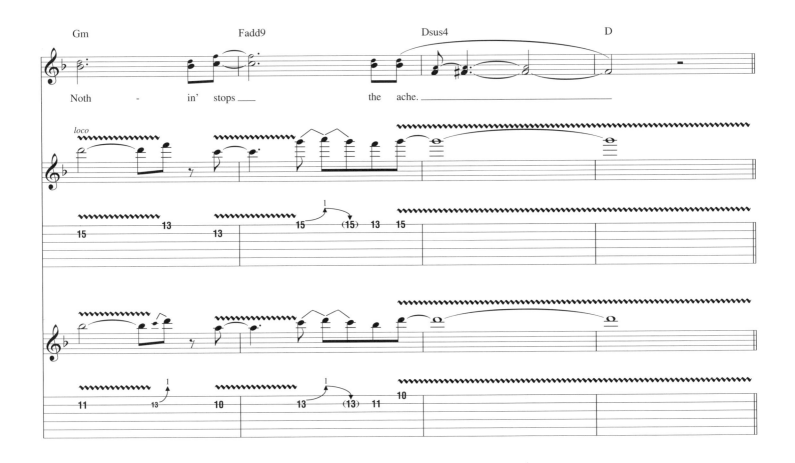

Noth - in' stops ___ the ache. ___

loco

Chorus

Gtr. 2: w/ Rhy. Fig. 3 (2 times)
Gtr. 3: w/ Rhy. Fig. 2 (4 times)
Gtrs. 5 & 6 tacet

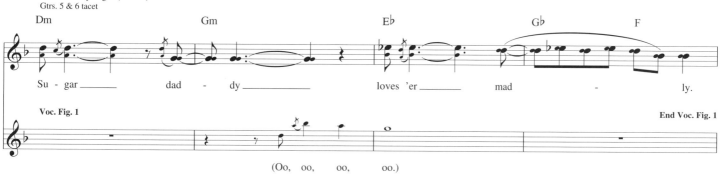

Su - gar _____ dad - dy _____ loves 'er _____ mad - ly.

(Oo, oo, oo, oo.)

Love 'er, _____ leave ___ 'er. _____ Mm, got off, _____ made ___ you a be - liev - er.

Ne - on _____ sol - dier _____ left her, now ___ you've got - ten old - er.

An - nie wants a ba - by now. ___ An - nie wants a ba - by an - y way ___ she can.

Outro

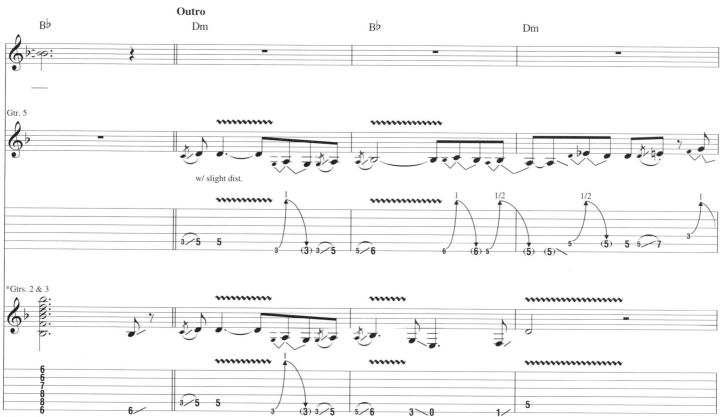

w/ slight dist.

Gtr. 5

*Gtrs. 2 & 3

*Composite arrangement

It's get - tin' long - er all the time.

It's time to re - de -sign the signs.

Oh, yeah.

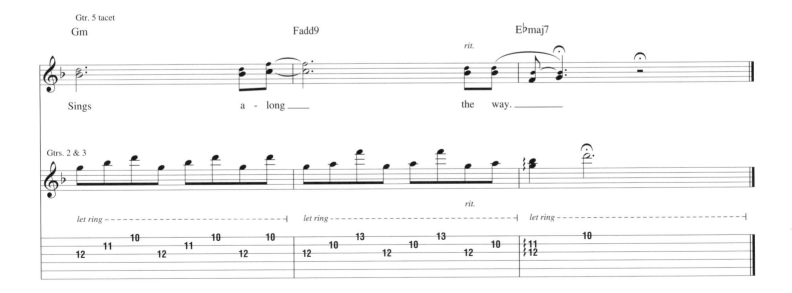

Sings a - long the way.

Look Around

Words and Music by Anthony Kiedis, Flea, Chad Smith and Josh Klinghoffer

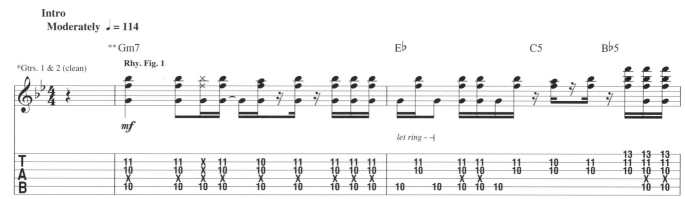

*Composite arrangement **Chord symbols reflect overall harmony.

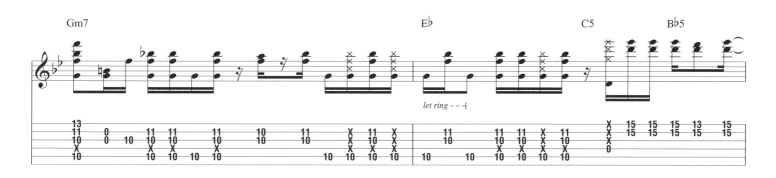

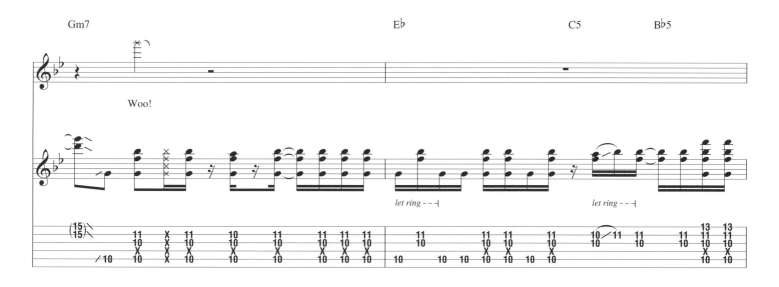

Verse

1. *Spoken:*
Stiff club, it's my na - ture. Cus - tom love is the no - men - cla - ture. Turn down mass con - fu - sion,

hit the road 'cause we just keep cruis - in'. Dou - ble my fun, dou - ble my vi - sion, long hard look at my last de - cis - ion.

Hus - tle here,___ hus - tle there.___ Hus - tle me, bitch, and you best be - ware.

*pp ___
w/ heavy reverb & ambient delay

*Vol. swell

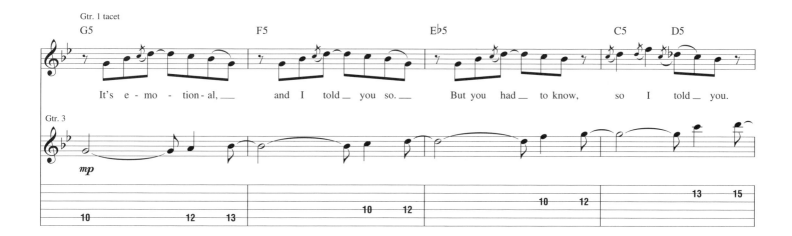

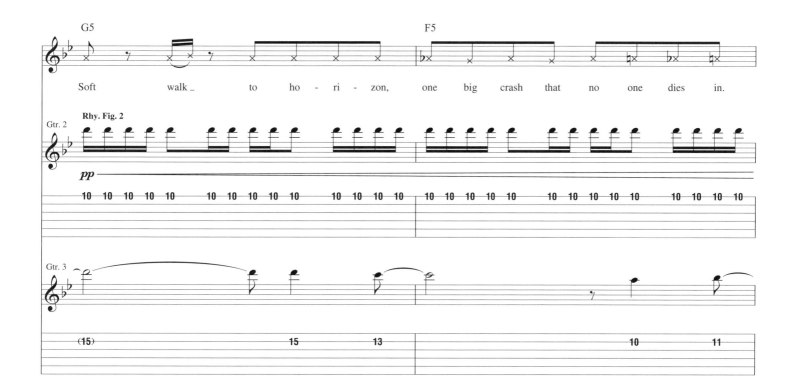

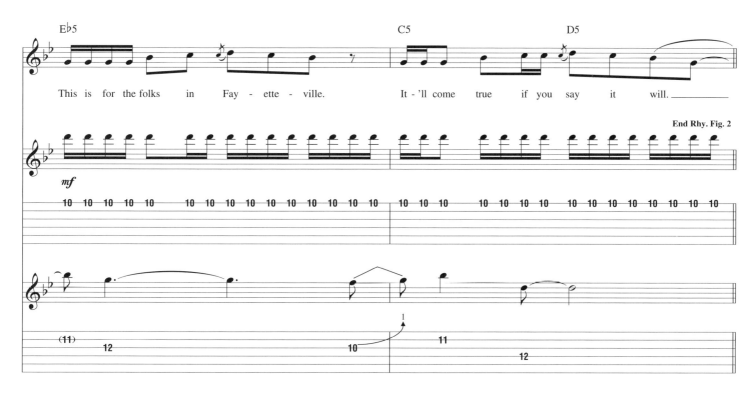

Verse

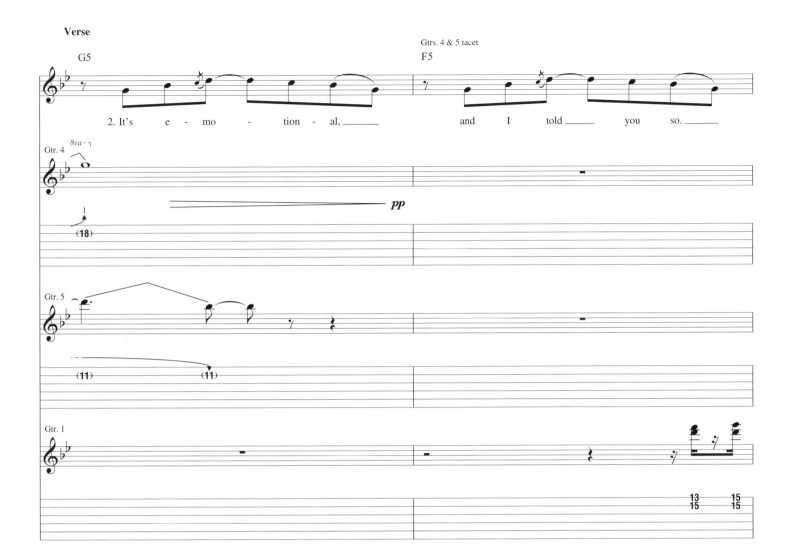

2. It's e - mo - tion - al, _____ and I told _____ you so. _____

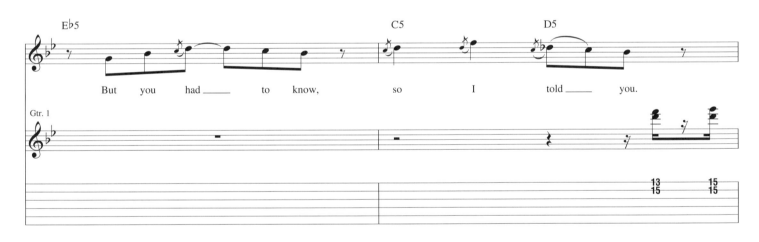

But you had _____ to know, so I told _____ you.

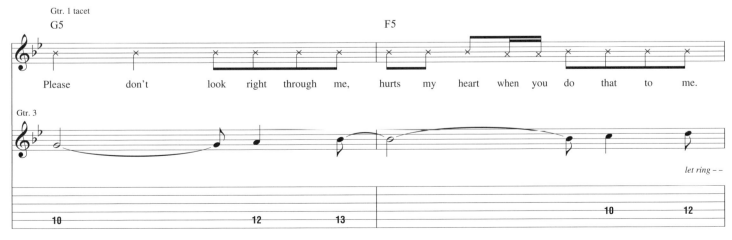

Please don't look right through me, hurts my heart when you do that to me.

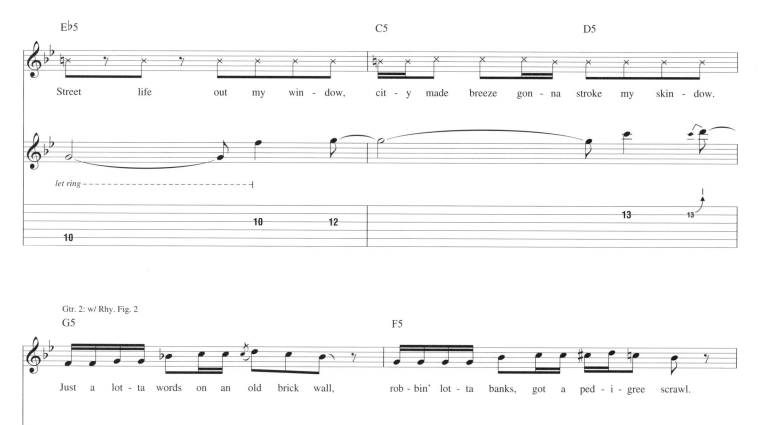

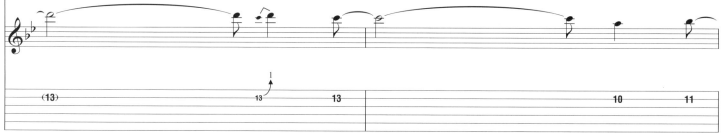

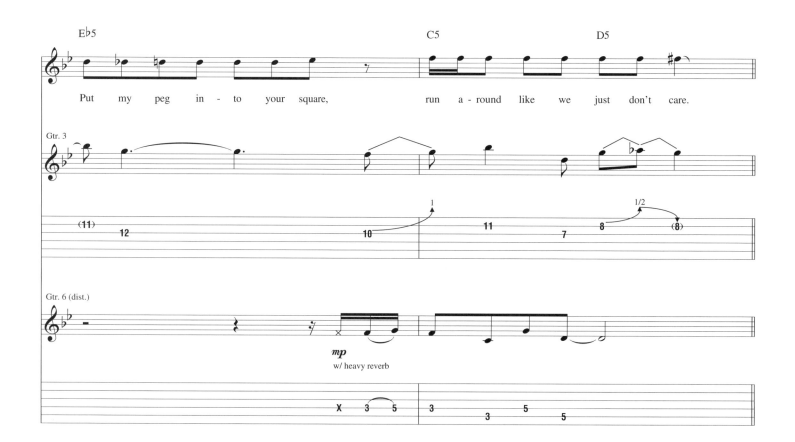

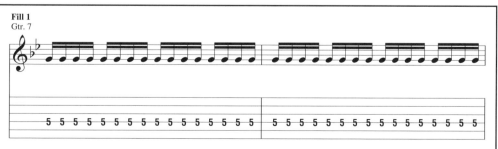

Oo, _____ oo.) _____

Bridge

Move it, I got, a get - cha, wan-na get - cha. Move it, I got, a get - cha, wan-na get - cha.

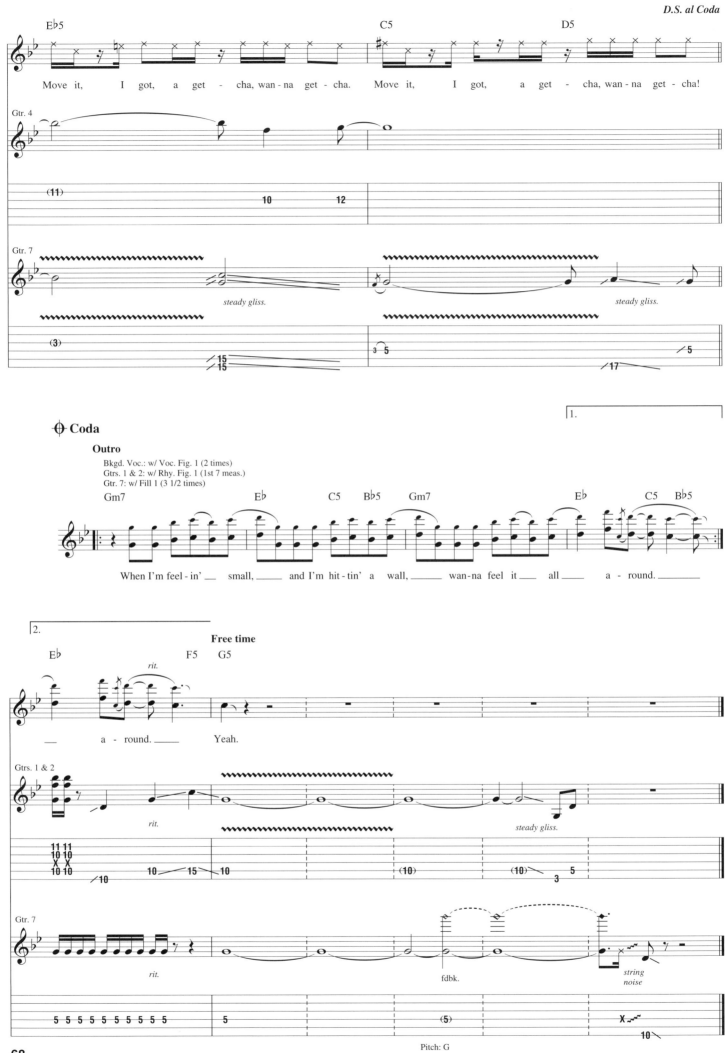

Coda

Outro

Bkgd. Voc.: w/ Voc. Fig. 1 (2 times)
Gtrs. 1 & 2: w/ Rhy. Fig. 1 (1st 7 meas.)
Gtr. 7: w/ Fill 1 (3 1/2 times)

When I'm feel-in' ___ small, ____ and I'm hit-tin' a wall, ____ wan-na feel it ___ all ___ a - round. ____

___ a - round. ____ Yeah.

Free time

Pitch: G

The Adventures of Rain Dance Maggie

Words and Music by Anthony Kiedis, Flea, Chad Smith and Josh Klinghoffer

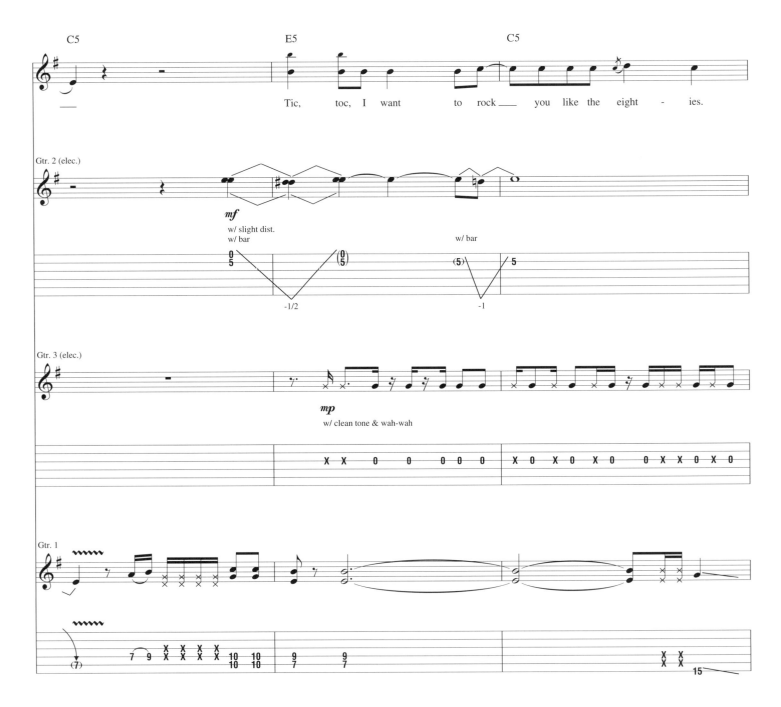

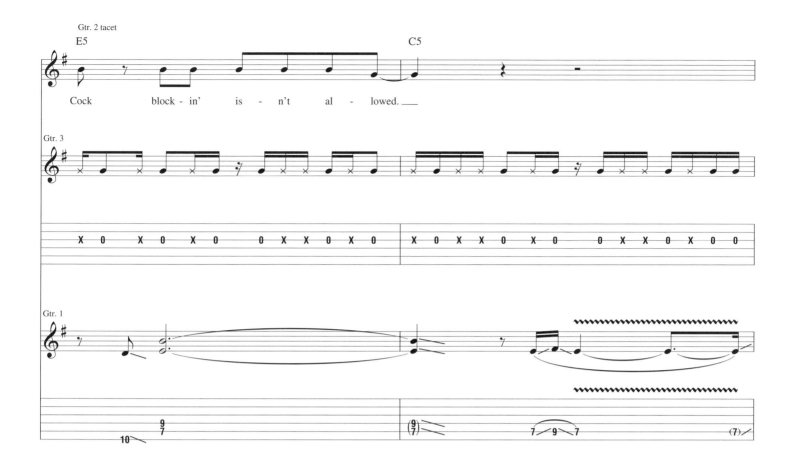

Gtr. 2 tacet

Cock block - in' is - n't al - lowed. __

Gtr. 3

Gtr. 1

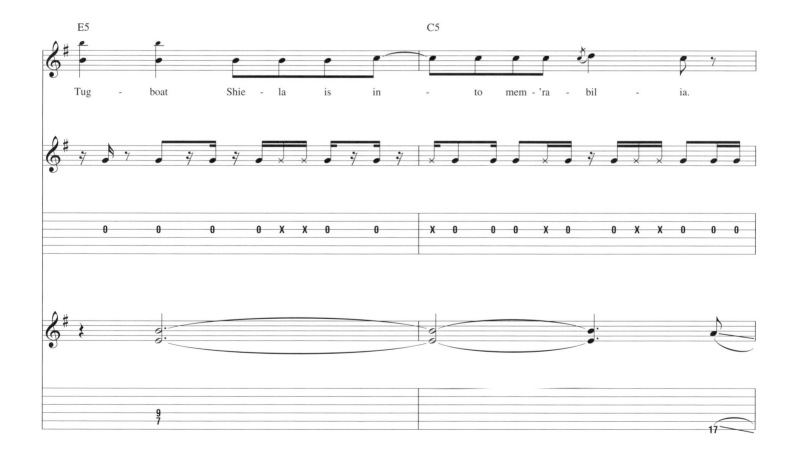

Tug - boat Shie - la is in - to mem - 'ra - bil - ia.

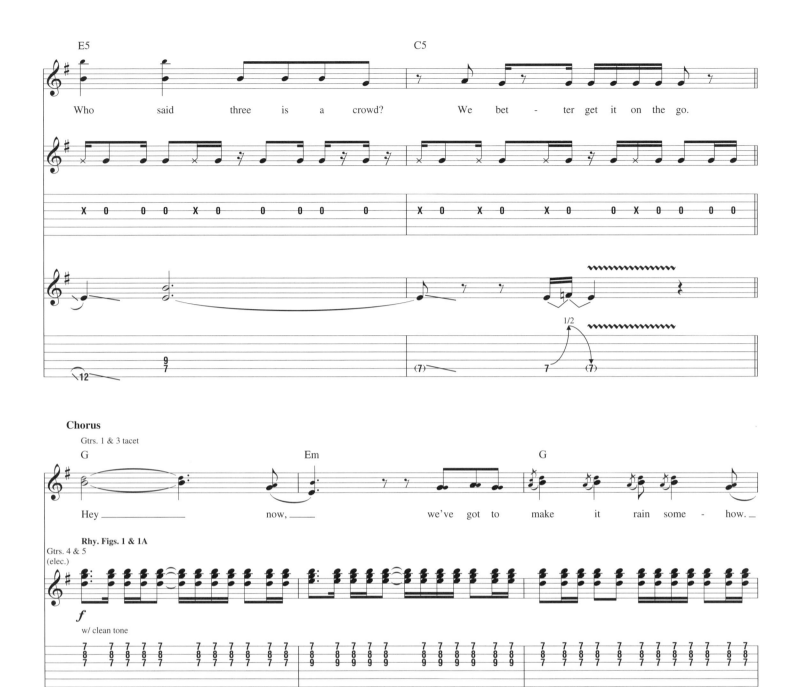

Chorus

Gtrs. 1 & 3 tacet

Rhy. Figs. 1 & 1A

Gtrs. 4 & 5
(elec.)

w/ clean tone

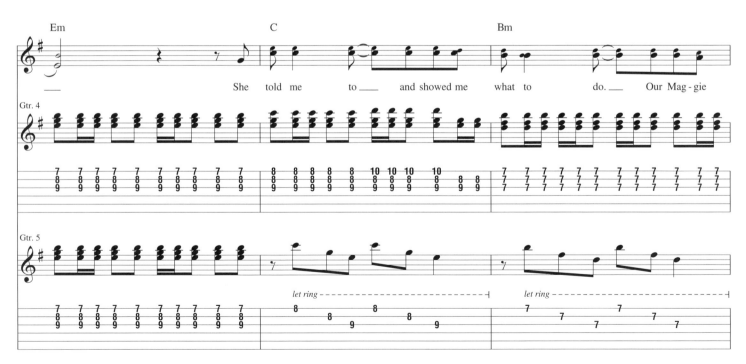

Gtr. 4

Gtr. 5

let ring -   let ring - - - - - - - - - - - - - - - - - - -

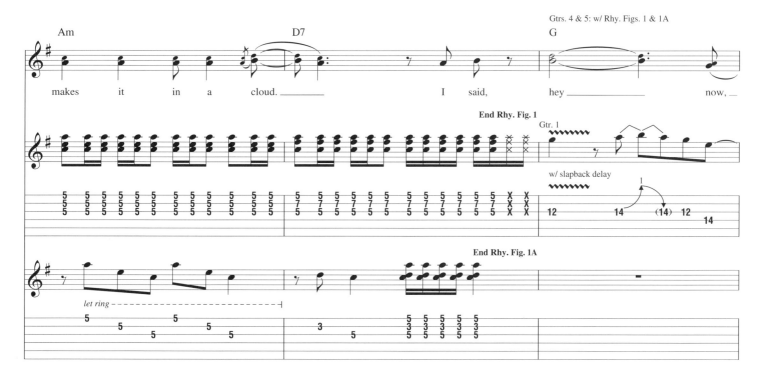

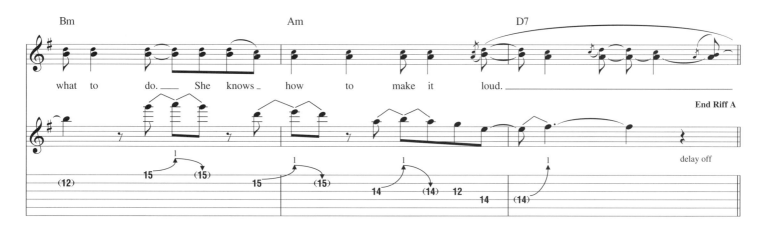

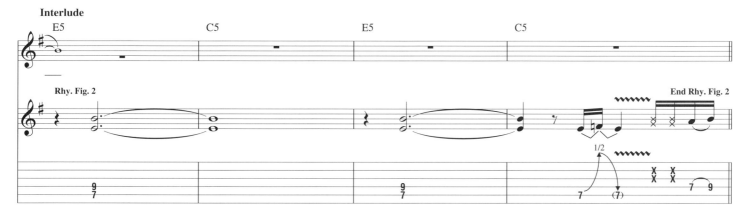

Verse

Gtr. 1: w/ Rhy. Fig. 2

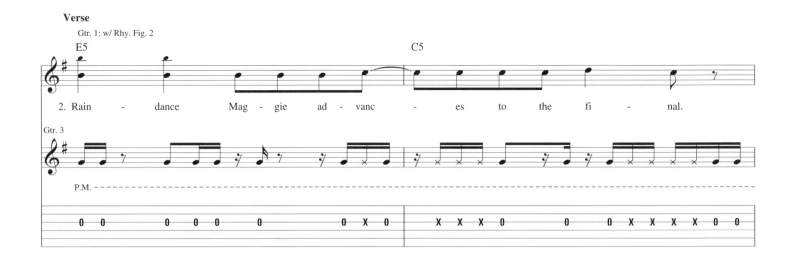

2. Rain - dance Mag - gie ad - vanc - es to the fi - nal.

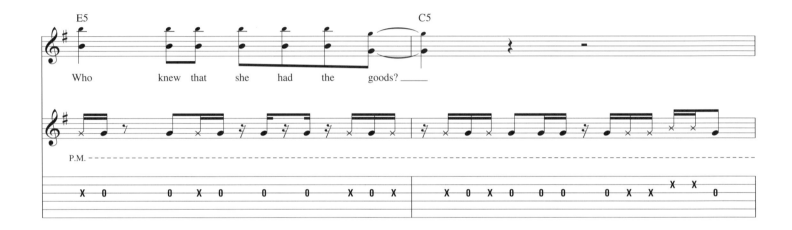

Who knew that she had the goods? ____

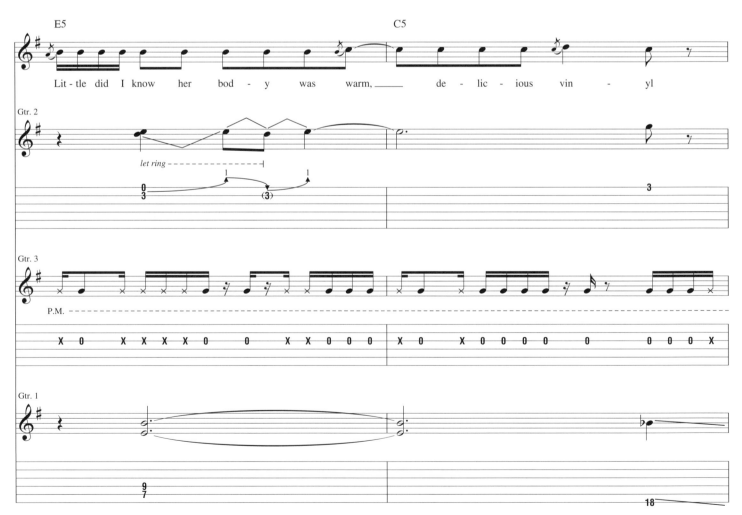

Lit - tle did I know her bod - y was warm, ____ de - lic - ious vin - yl

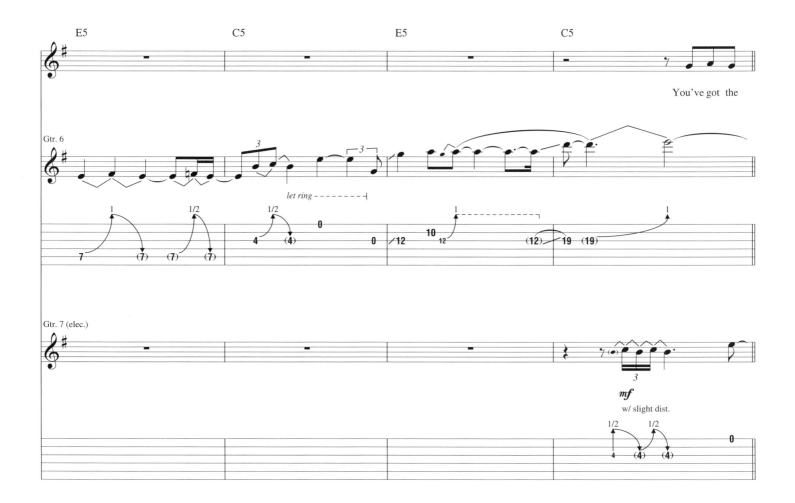

You've got the

Bridge

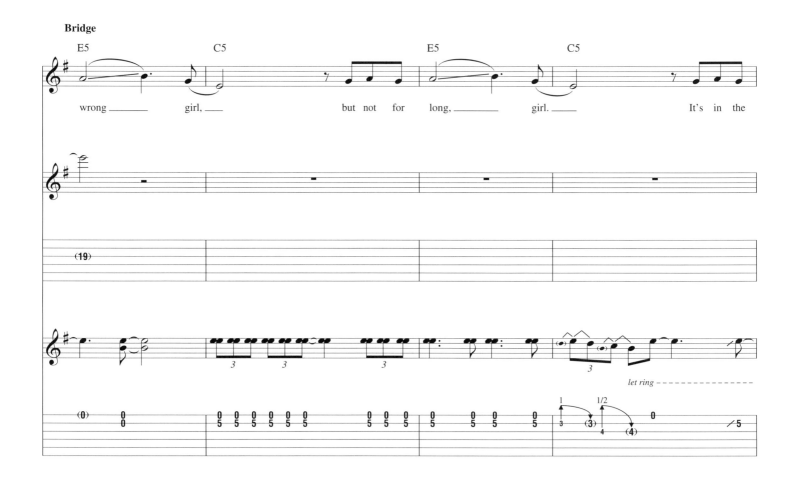

wrong _____ girl, _____ but not for long, _____ girl. _____ It's in the

76

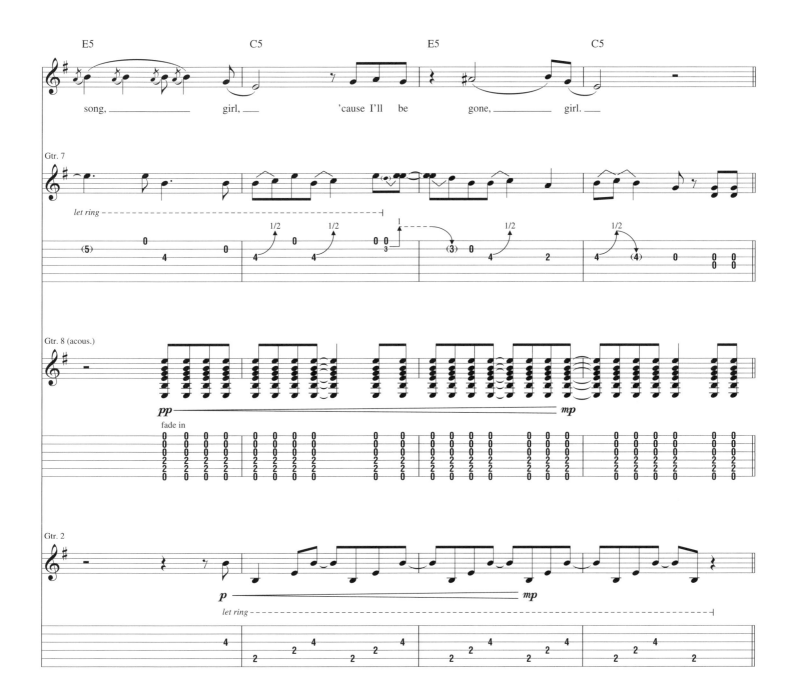

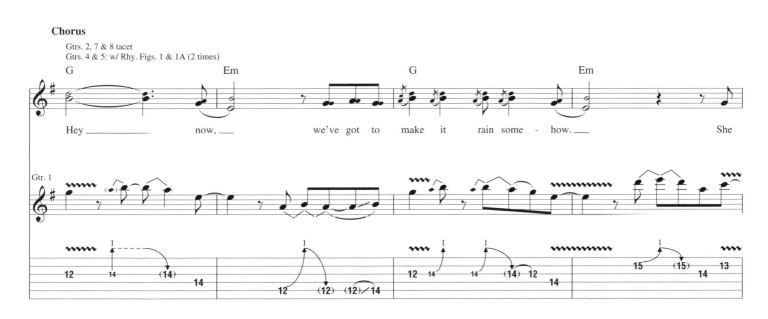

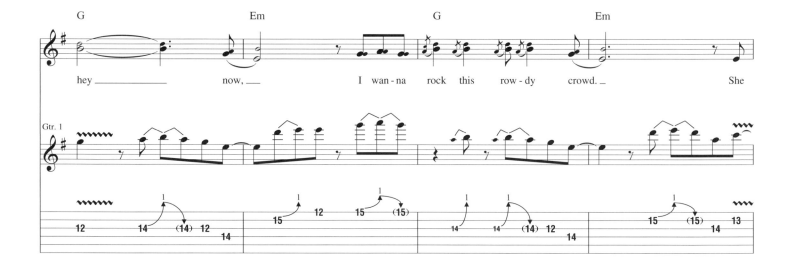

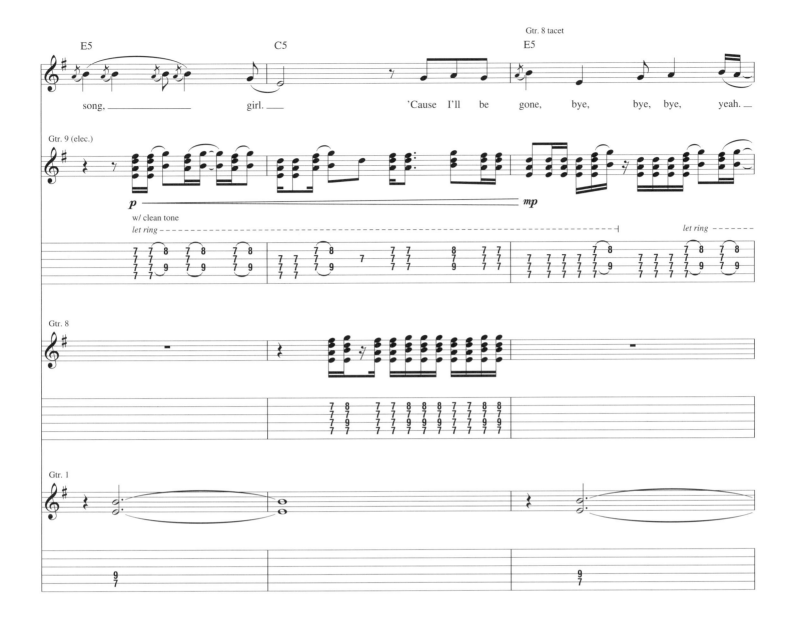

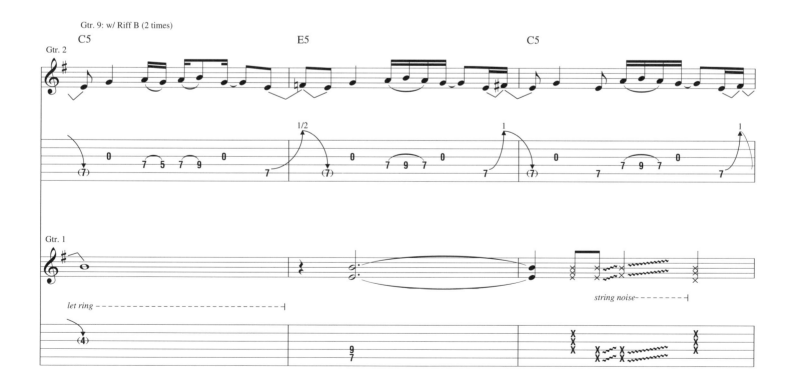

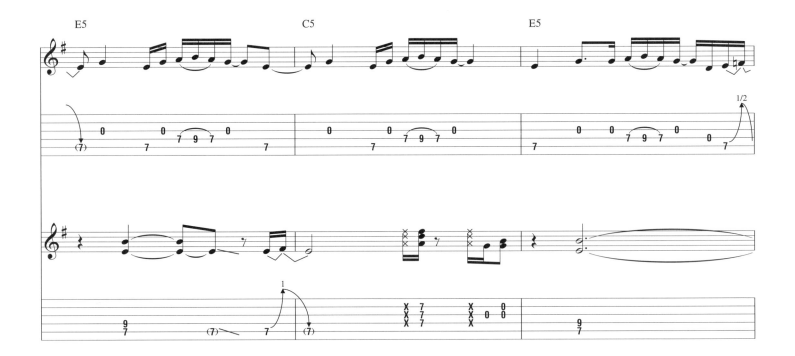

Did I Let You Know

Words and Music by Anthony Kiedis, Flea, Chad Smith and Josh Klinghoffer

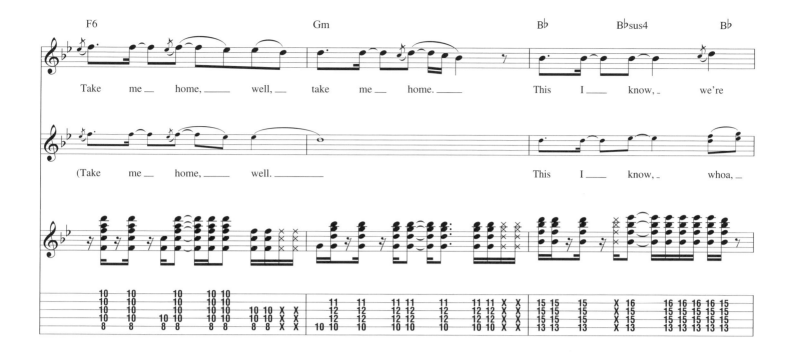

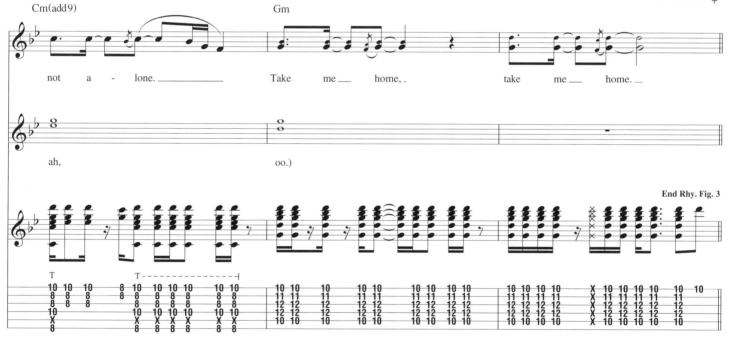

Trumpet Solo

Cm7

Gtrs. 1 & 2

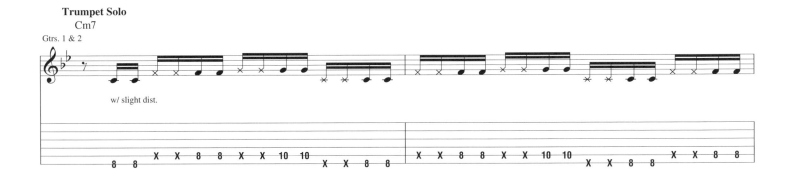

w/ slight dist.

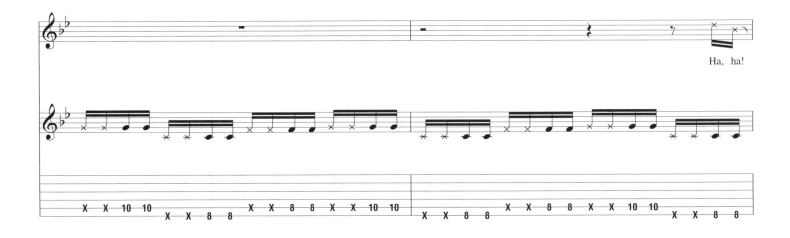

Ha, ha!

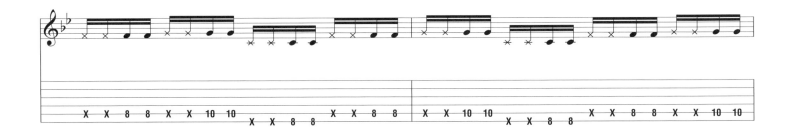

dist. off

Verse

Gtrs. 1 & 2: w/ Rhy. Figs. 1 & 1A

Cm(add9)   B♭   B♭sus4   B♭   B♭add9

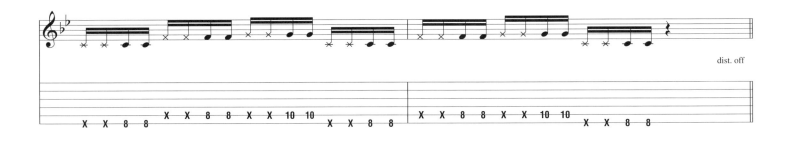

3. I'm com-in' at you._ Well,   year of the cat, too,_ and   I like the sound of your ar - tic - u - la - tions.

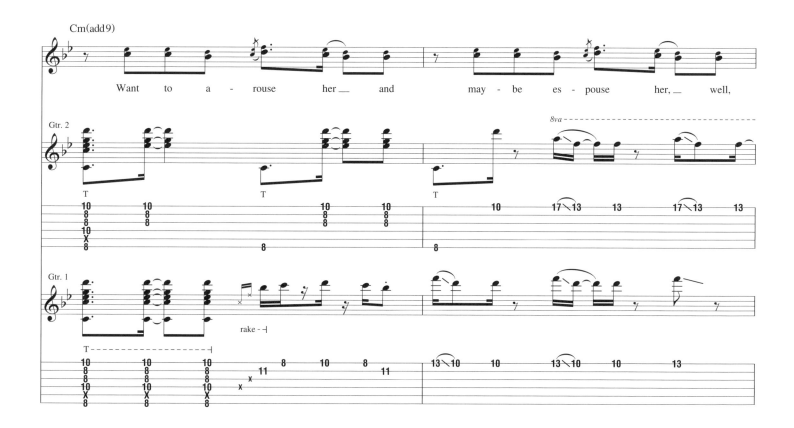

Want to a - rouse her ___ and may - be es - pouse her, ___ well,

D.S. al Coda 1

Gtr. 1: w/ Rhy. Fig. 1 (last 2 meas.)

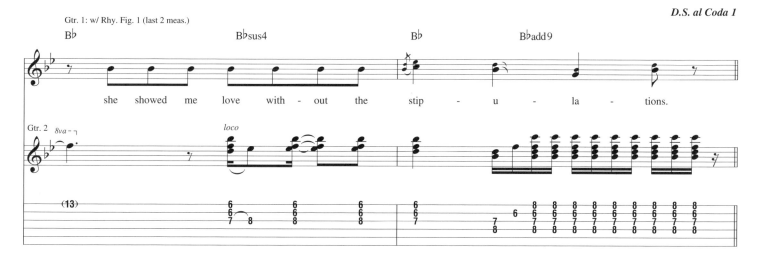

she showed me love with - out the stip - u - la - tions.

⊕ Coda 1
Guitar Solo

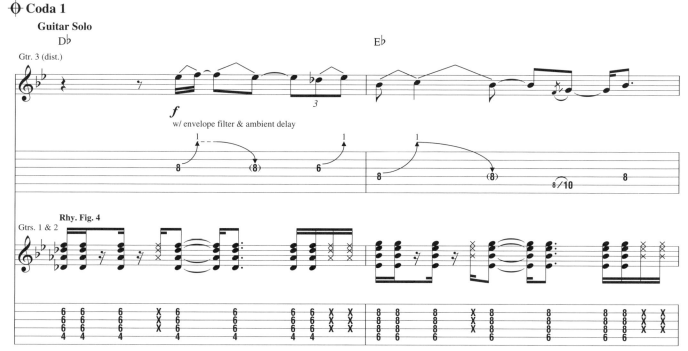

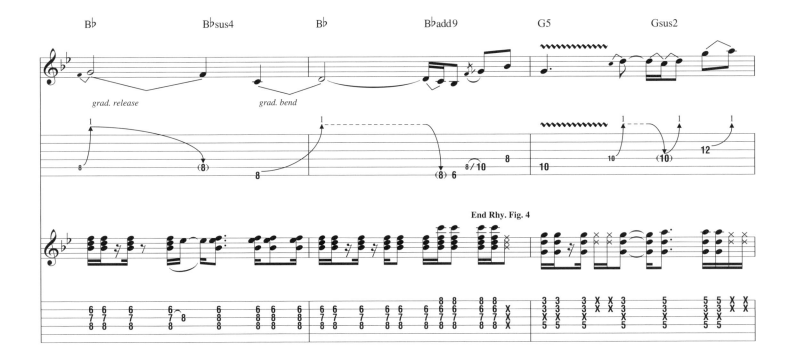

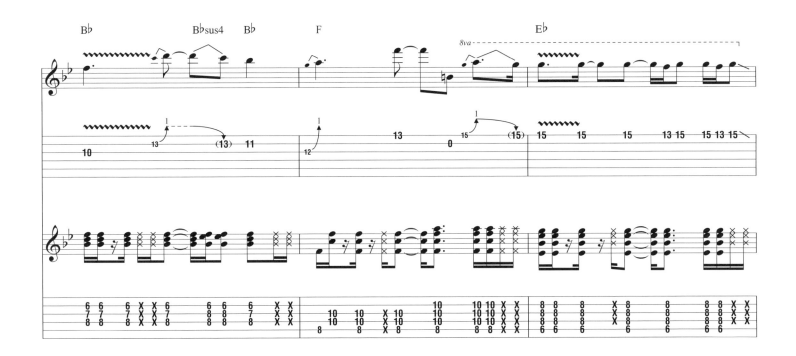

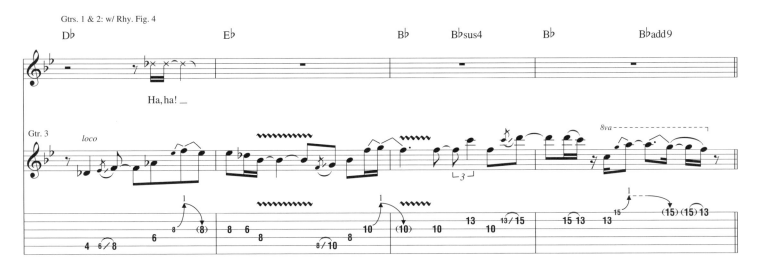

Verse

Gtr. 1: w/ Rhy. Fig. 1
Gtr. 2: w/ Rhy. Fig. 1A (2 times)

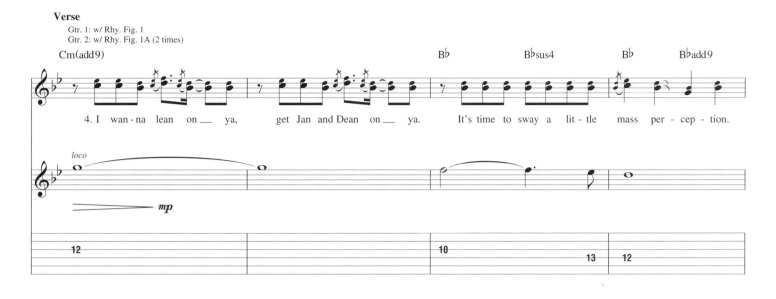

4. I wan-na lean on __ ya, get Jan and Dean on __ ya. It's time to sway a lit-tle mass per-cep-tion.

D.S. al Coda 2

Gtr. 1: w/ Rhy. Fig. 2

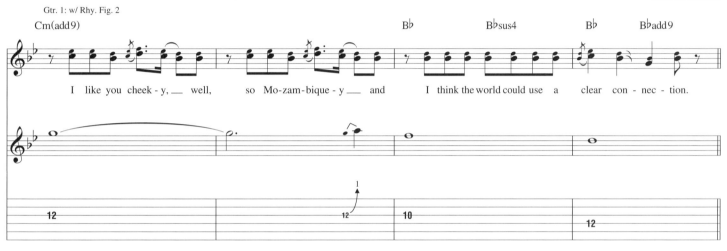

I like you cheek-y, __ well, so Mo-zam-bique-y __ and I think the world could use a clear con-nec-tion.

⊕ Coda 2

Chorus

Gtrs. 1 & 2: w/ Rhy. Fig. 3

This I __ know, __ yeah, this I __ know. __ Take me __ home, __ well, __ take me __ home. __

(Take me __ home, __ well. __

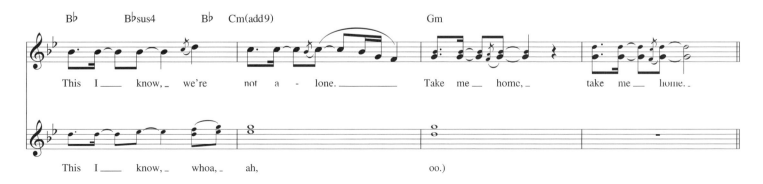

This I __ know, __ we're not a - lone. __ Take me __ home, __ take me __ home. __

This I __ know, __ whoa, __ ah, oo.)

89

Outro

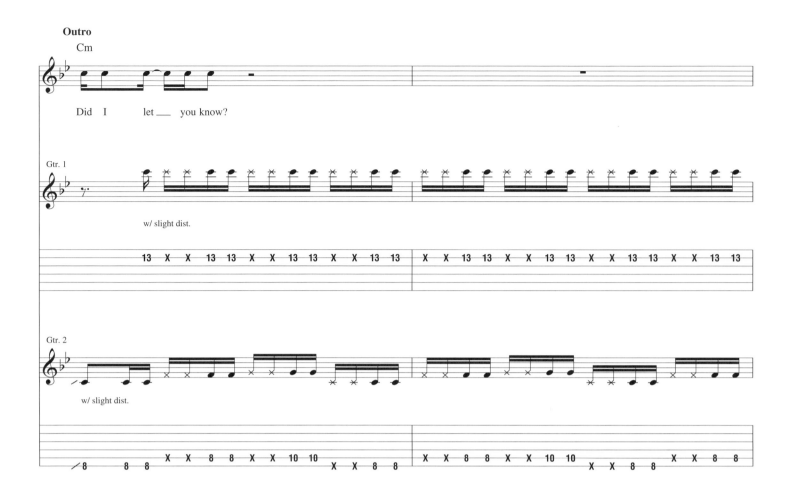

Did I   let ___ you know?

Gtr. 1

w/ slight dist.

Gtr. 2

w/ slight dist.

B♭

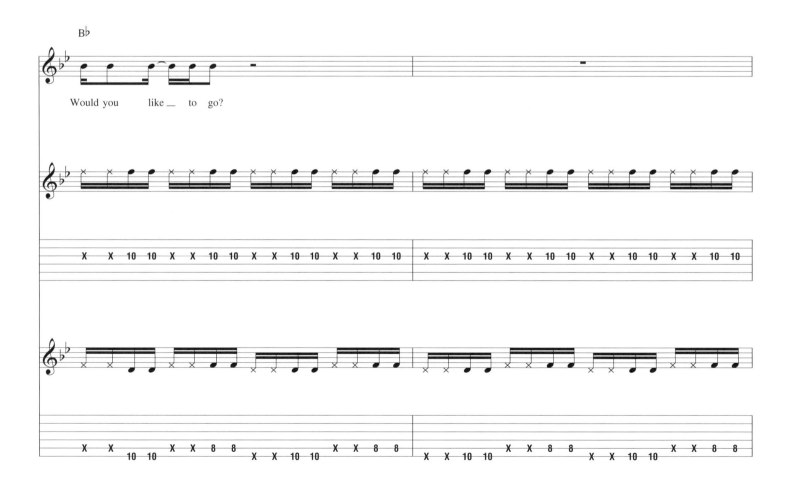

Would you   like ___ to go?

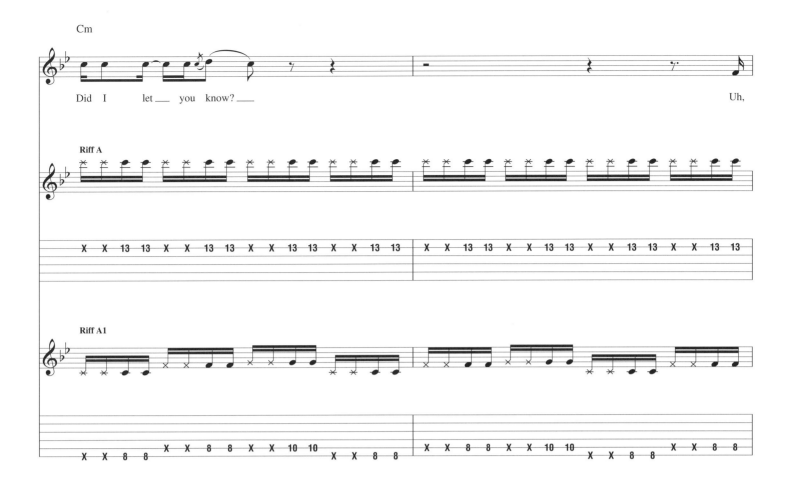

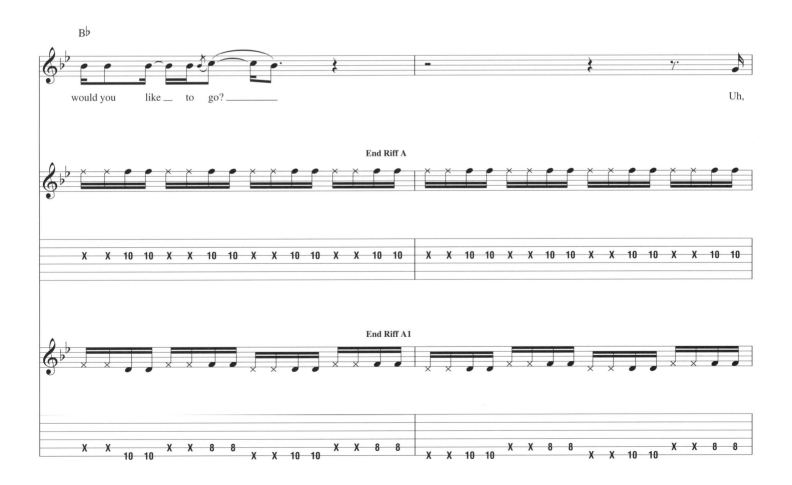

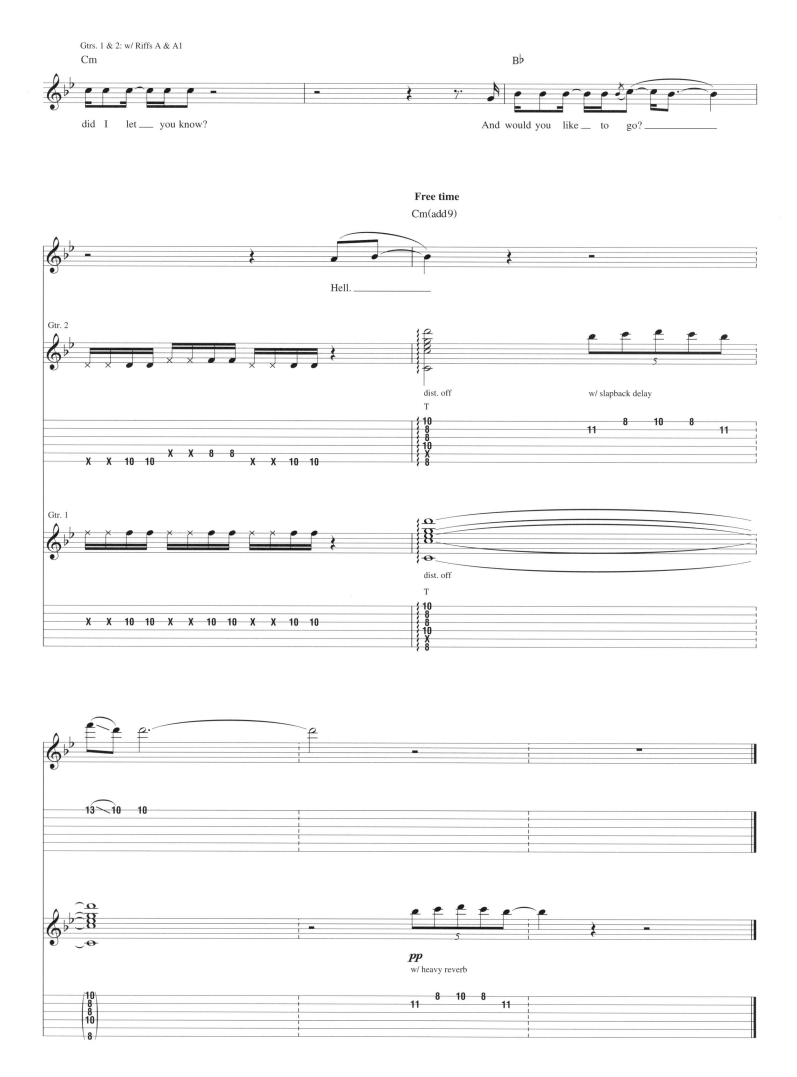

Goodbye Hooray

Words and Music by Anthony Kiedis, Flea, Chad Smith and Josh Klinghoffer

*See top of page for chord diagrams pertaining to rhythm slashes.

Whispered: Chi-ga, chi-ga, chi-ga, chi.

Verse

Gtr. 1: w/ Rhy. Fig. 1 (2 times)

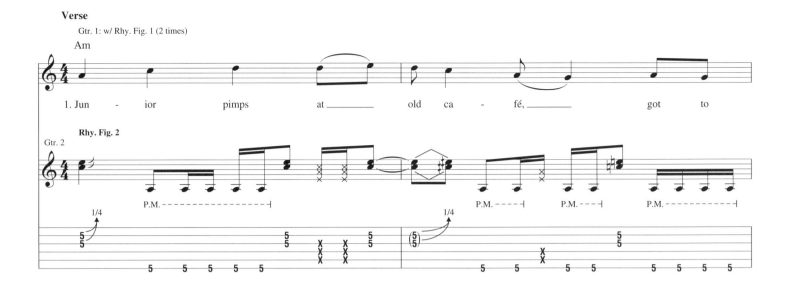

1. Jun - ior pimps at ____ old ca - fé, ____ got to

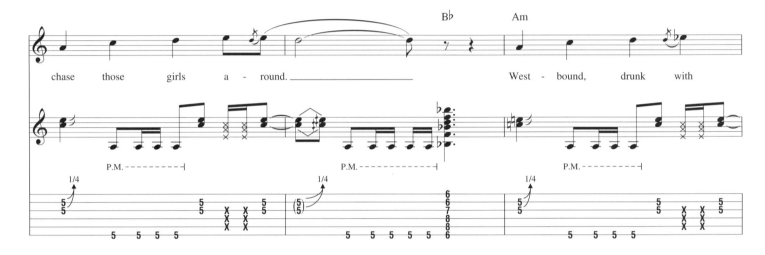

chase those girls a - round. ____ West - bound, drunk with

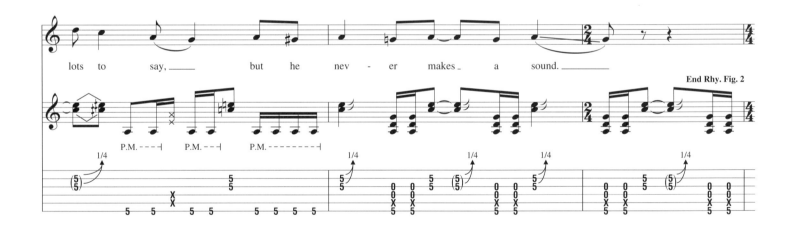

lots to say, ____ but he nev - er makes ____ a sound. ____

Gtr. 2: w/ Rhy. Fig. 2

Hus - tlers get what ____ they de - serve, ____ but it's al - ways half the gate. ____

Good things come to ____ those who wait, ____ like an ex - pi - ra - tion date. ____

94

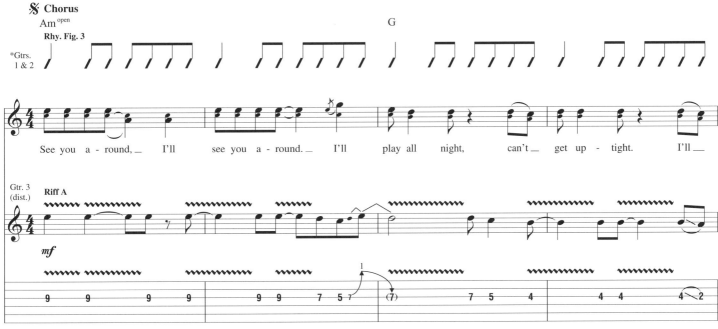

*Gtrs. 1 & 2

See you a - round, __ I'll see you a - round. __ I'll play all night, can't __ get up - tight. I'll __

*Composite arrangement

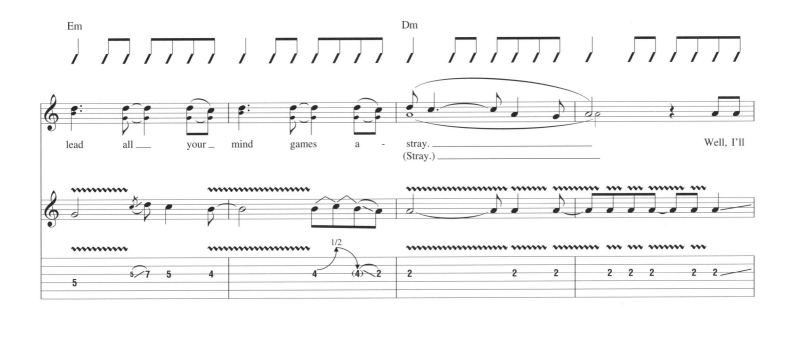

lead all __ your __ mind games a - stray. _____

(Stray.) _____

Well, I'll

see you a - round, __ I'll see you a - round. __ I'll play all night, can't __ get up - tight. See __

you, so long, good-bye, hoo-ray.
(Ray.)

Oh!

Guitar Solo

Gtr. 1: w/ Rhy. Fig. 1
Gtr. 2: w/ Rhy. Fig. 2

Oh, hey, hey!

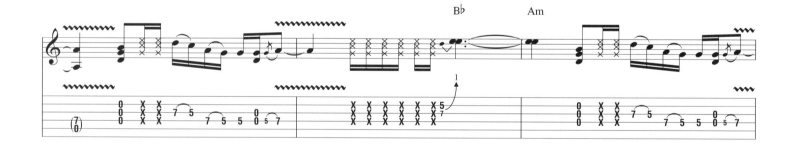

Verse

Gtr. 1: w/ Rhy. Fig. 1
Gtr. 2: w/ Rhy. Fig. 2

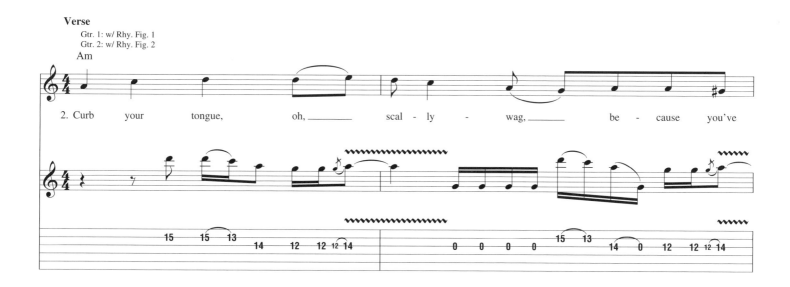

2. Curb your tongue, oh, _____ scal - ly - wag, _____ be - cause you've

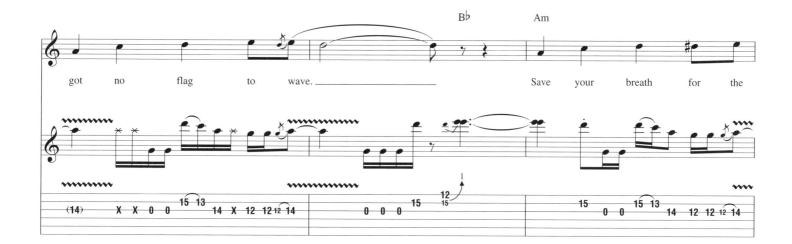

got no flag to wave. _____ Save your breath for the

black and white. _____ Ev - 'ry dog will have _____ his day. _____

Chorus

Gtrs. 1 & 2: w/ Rhy. Fig. 3
Gtr. 3: w/ Riff A

See you a - round, _____ I'll see you a - round. _____ I'll play all night, can't _____ get up - tight. I'll _____

lead all __ your __ mind games a - stray, _____ yeah. _____ Well, I'll
(Stray.)

see you a - round, _ I'll see you a - round. __ I'll play all night, can't __ get up - tight see __

you, so long, __ good - bye, __ hoo - ray. _____ Well, I'll
(Ray.) _____

see you a - round, ____ I'll see you a - round. _____
(See you a - round. ____ I'll see you a - round.) _____

Bass Solo

Gtrs. 1 & 2: w/ Rhy. Fig. 1 (2 times)
Gtr. 3 tacet

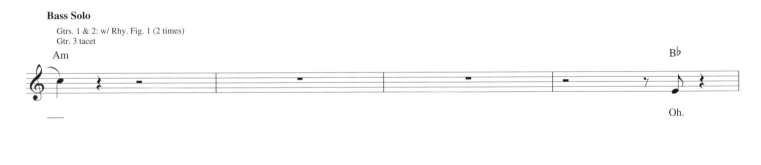

Oh.

Oo!

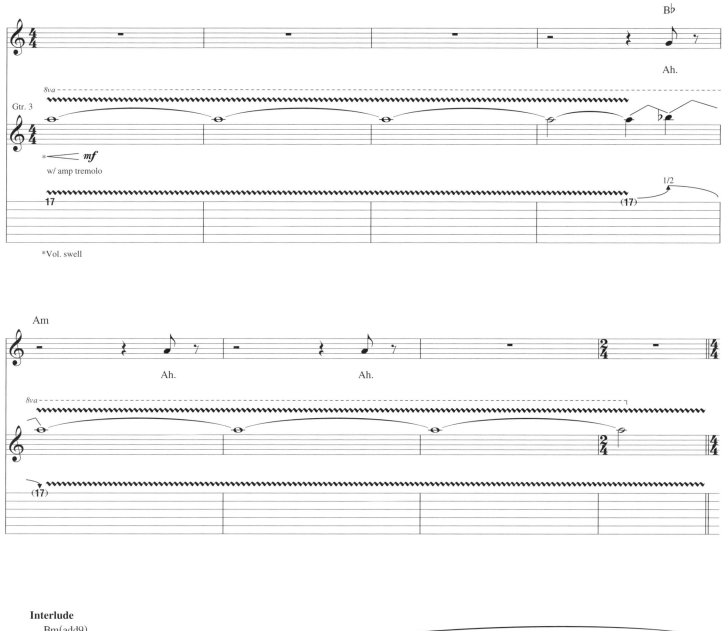

*Vol. swell

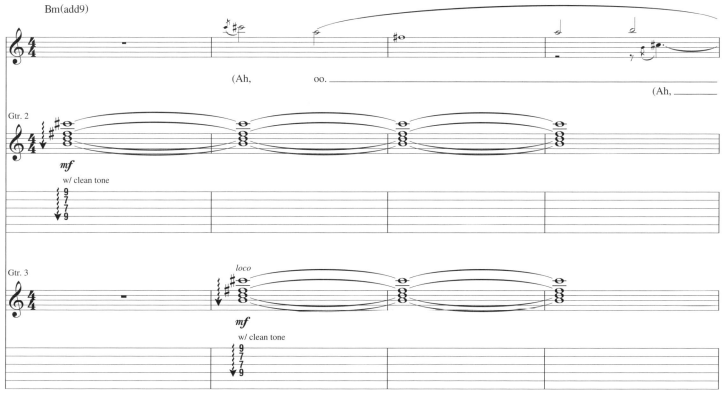

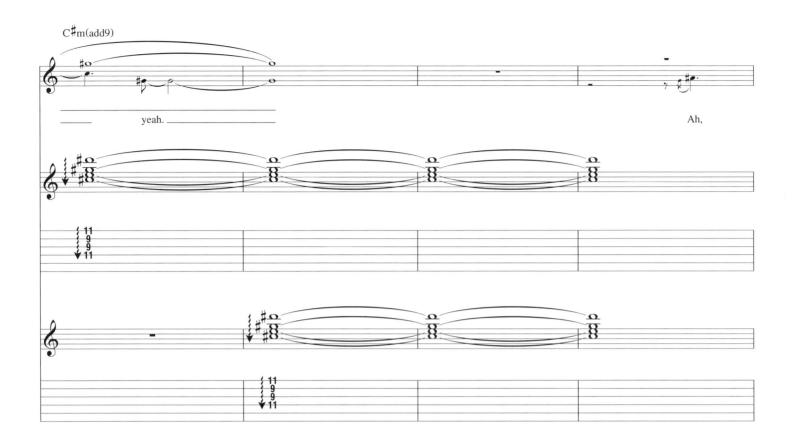

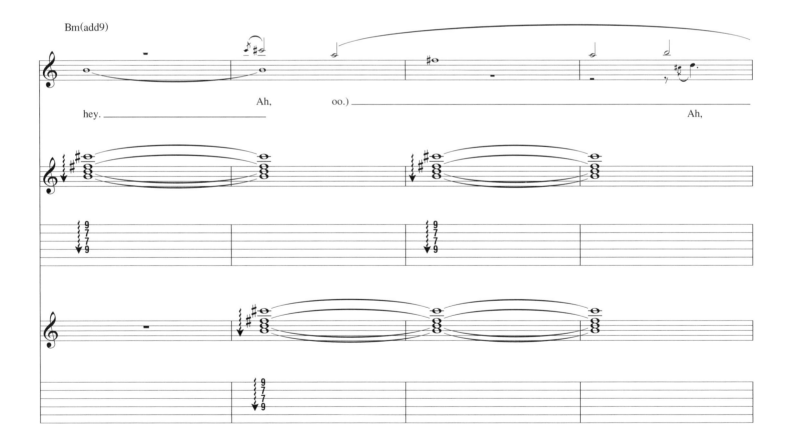

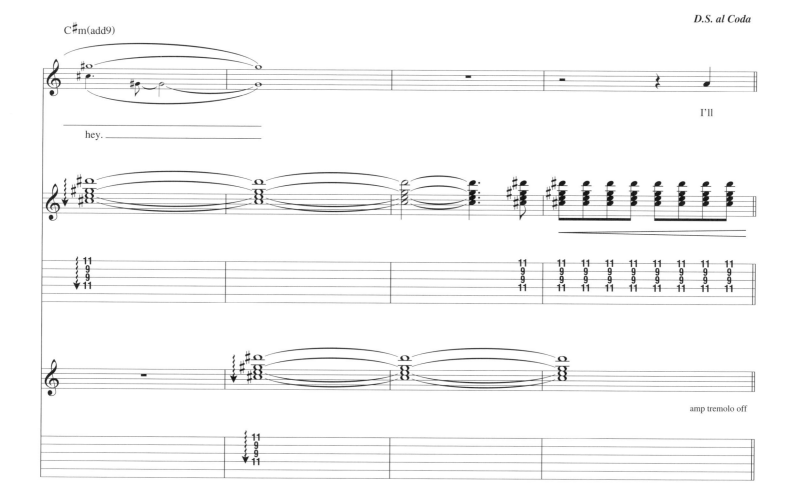

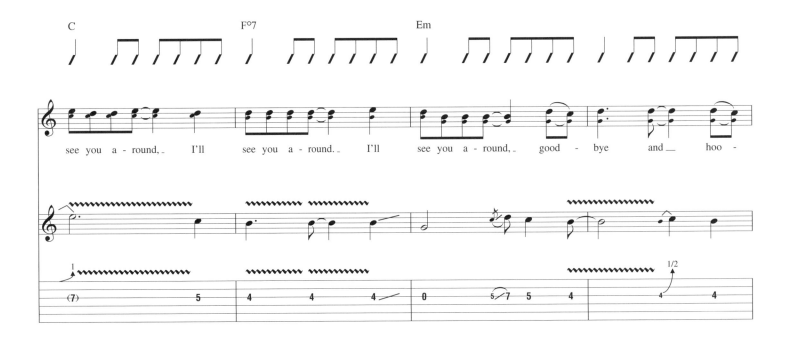

see you a - round, I'll see you a - round. I'll see you a - round, good - bye and hoo -

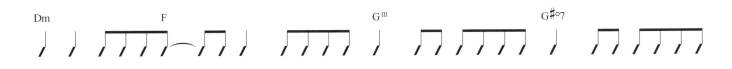

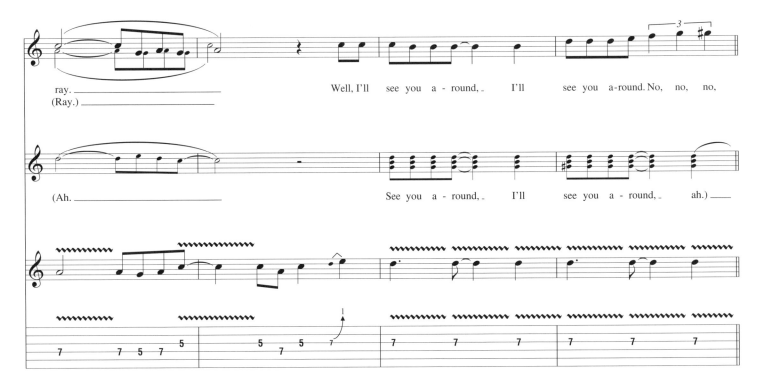

ray.
(Ray.)

Well, I'll see you a - round, I'll see you a-round. No, no, no,

(Ah.

See you a - round, I'll see you a - round, ah.)

Outro-Guitar Solo

Gtr. 1: w/ Rhy. Fig. 1 (2 times)
Gtr. 2: w/ Rhy. Fig. 1A (1 3/4 times)

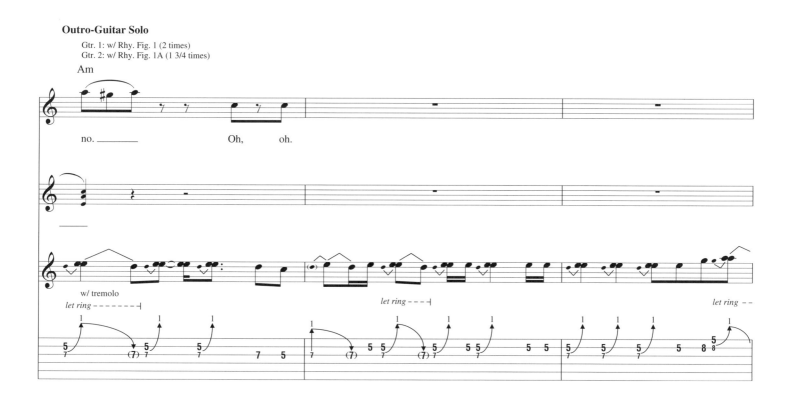

no. _____ Oh, oh.

w/ tremolo

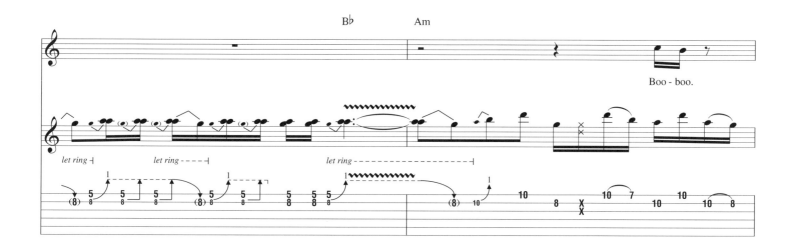

Boo - boo.

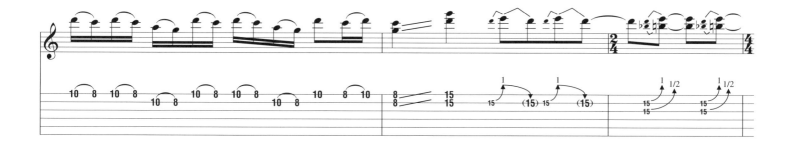

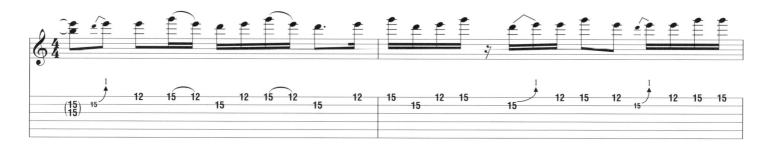

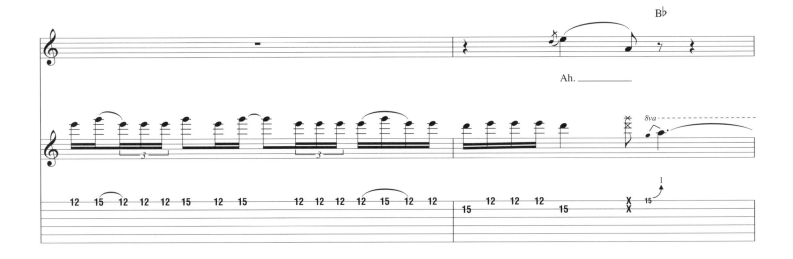

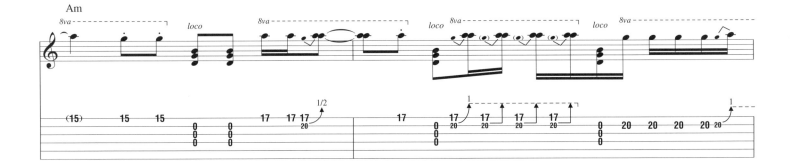

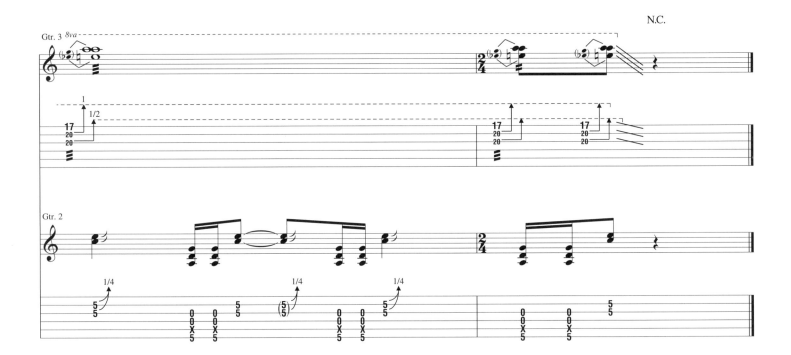

Happiness Loves Company

Words and Music by Anthony Kiedis, Flea, Chad Smith and Josh Klinghoffer

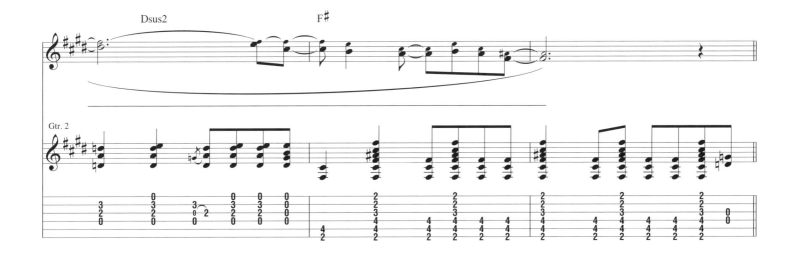

Bridge

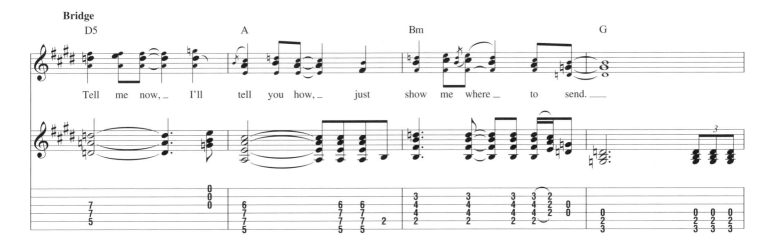

Tell me now, __ I'll tell you how, __ just show me where __ to send. __

𝄋 Chorus

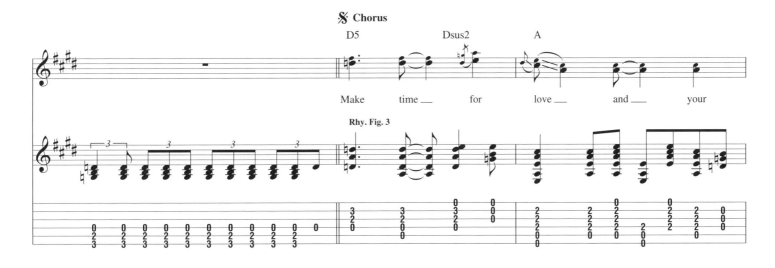

Make time __ for love __ and __ your

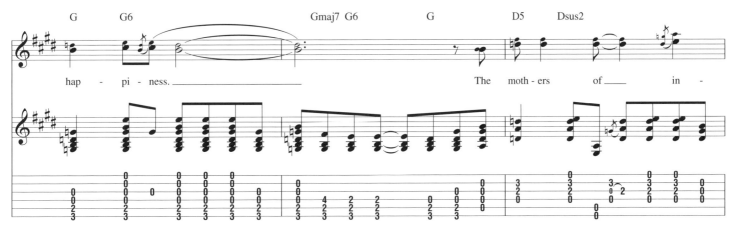

hap - pi - ness. _____ The moth - ers of __ in -

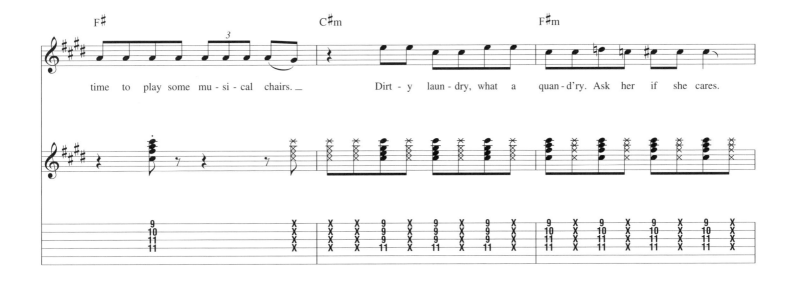

time to play some mu-si-cal chairs. __ Dirt-y laun-dry, what a quan-d'ry. Ask her if she cares.

I'll be yours and more, bet-ter than ev-er like nev-er be-fore.

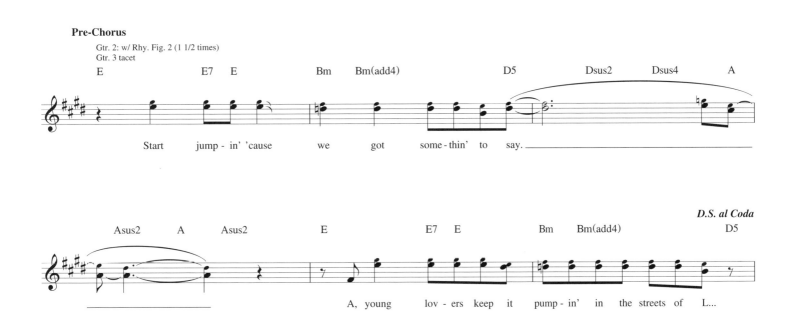

Pre-Chorus

Gtr. 2: w/ Rhy. Fig. 2 (1 1/2 times)
Gtr. 3 tacet

Start jump-in' 'cause we got some-thin' to say. __

D.S. al Coda

A, young lov-ers keep it pump-in' in the streets of L...

Police Station

Words and Music by Anthony Kiedis, Flea, Chad Smith and Josh Klinghoffer

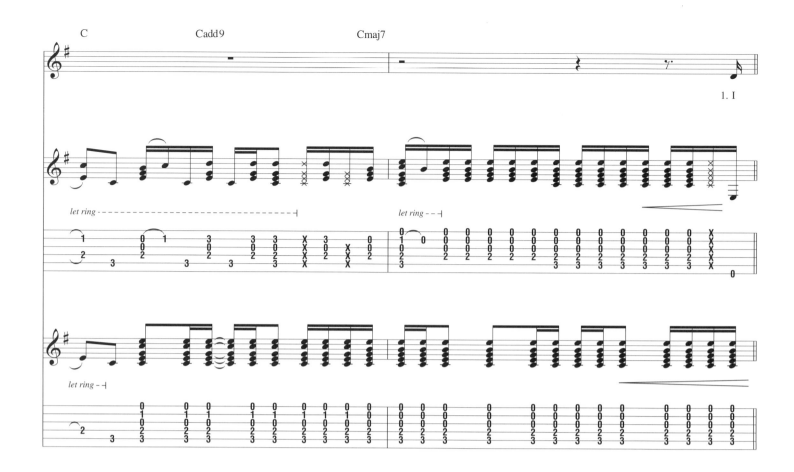

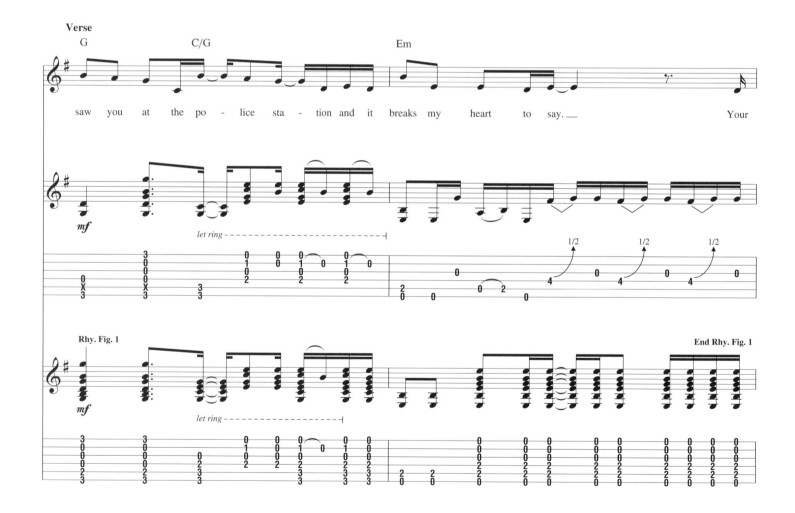

saw you at the po-lice sta-tion and it breaks my heart to say.___ Your

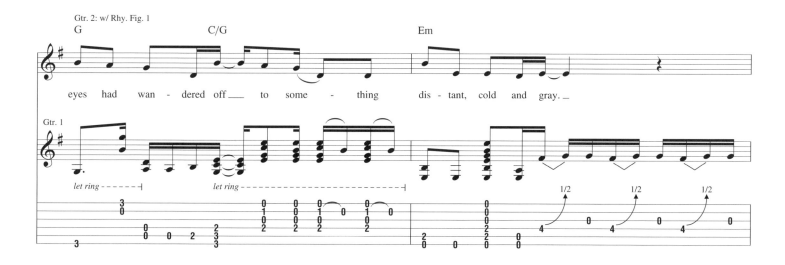

eyes had wan - dered off ___ to some - thing dis - tant, cold and gray. ___

I guess you did - n't see it com - ing, ___ some-one's got used to slum - ming.

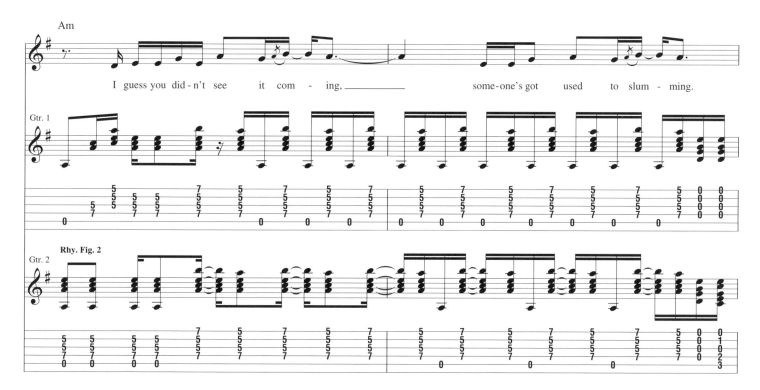

Dream-in' of the gold - en years, ___ I see you had to change ca - reers. ___ Far

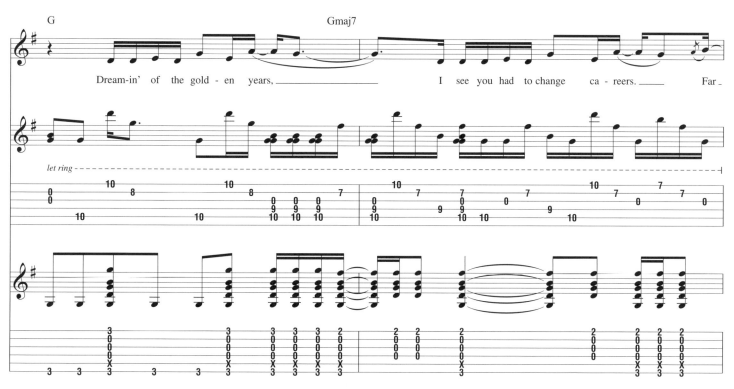

Gtr. 2: w/ Rhy. Fig. 2

Am

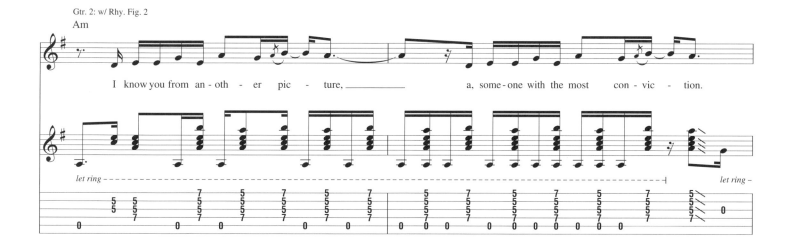

I know you from an - oth - er pic - ture, _____ a, some - one with the most con - vic - tion.

let ring - *let ring* -

G   Gmaj7

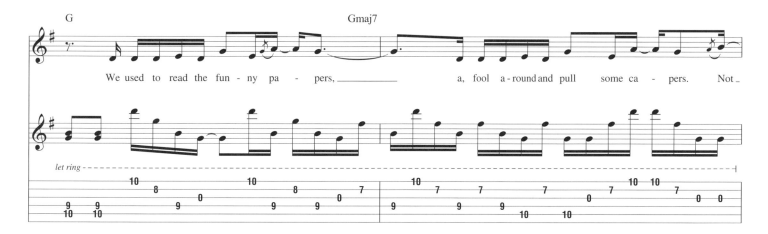

We used to read the fun - ny pa - pers, _____ a, fool a - round and pull some ca - pers. Not __

let ring -

Am

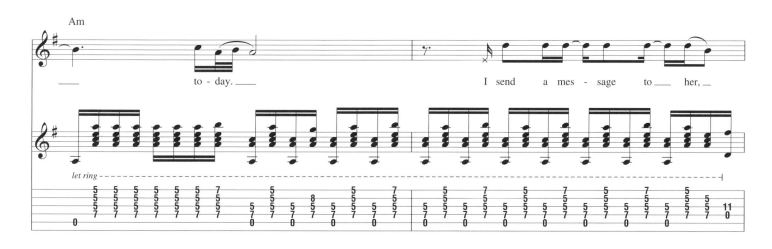

__ to - day. ____   I send a mes - sage to __ her, __

let ring -

*D

Gtr. 2

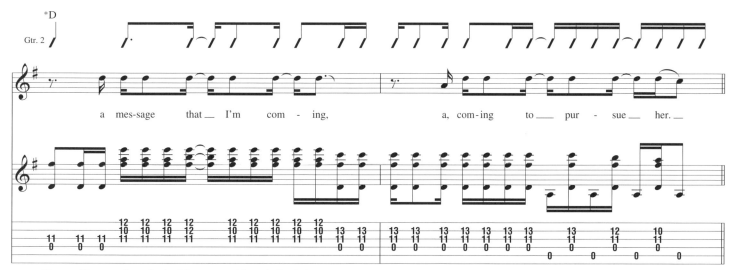

a mes - sage that __ I'm com - ing, a, com - ing to __ pur - sue her.

*See top of first page of song for chord diagrams pertaining to rhythm slashes.

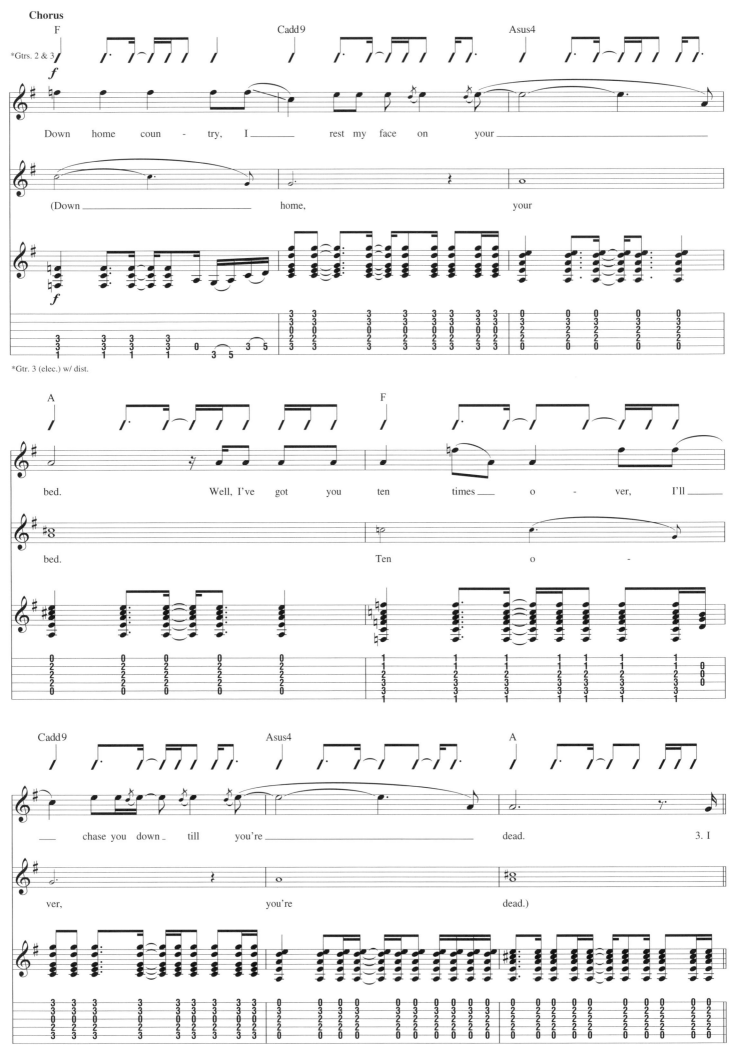

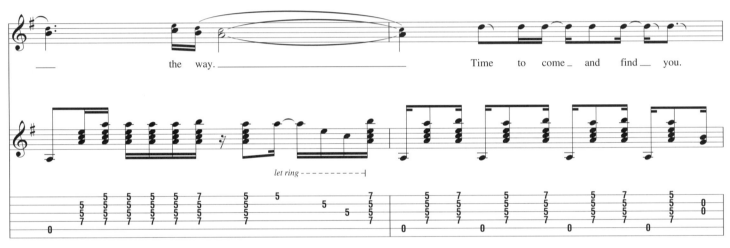

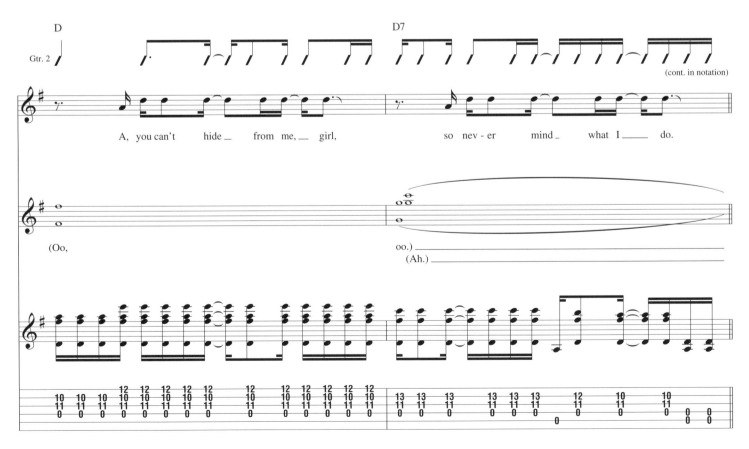

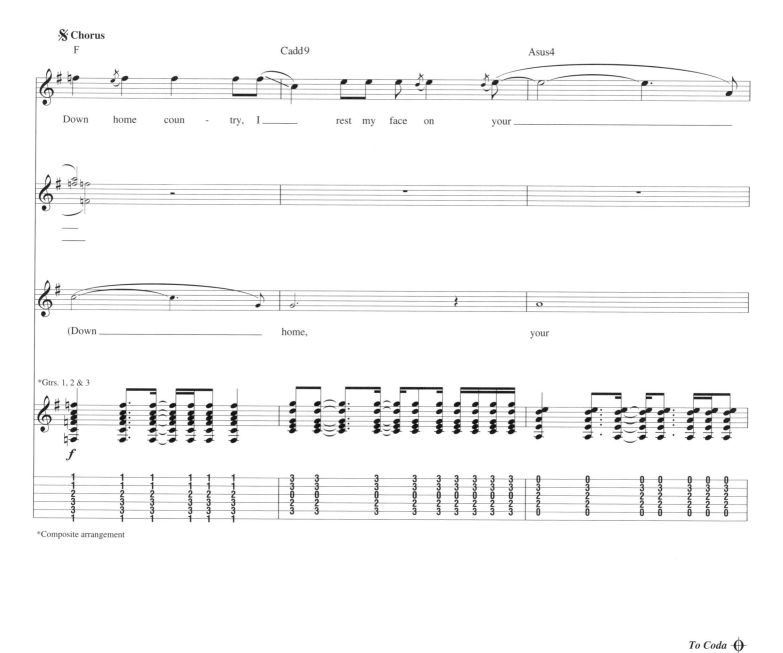

*Composite arrangement

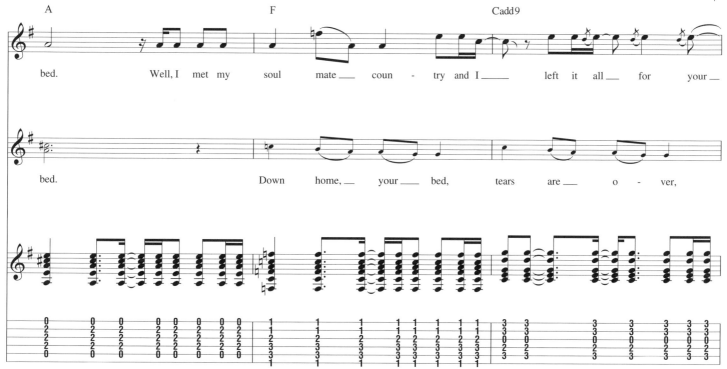

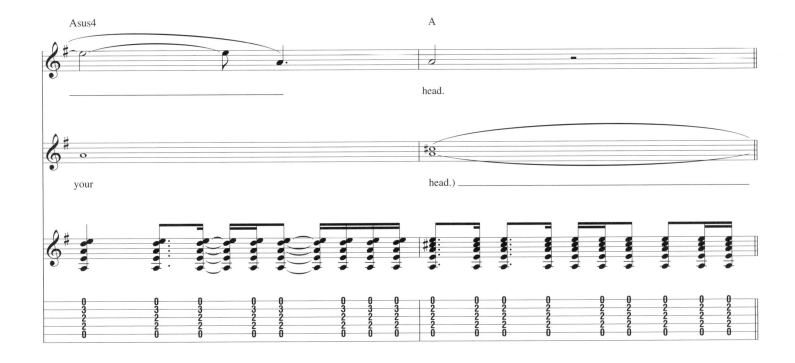

Interlude

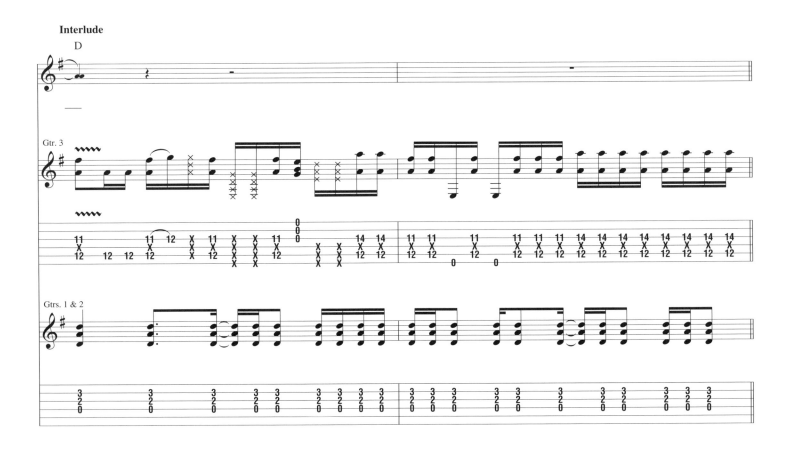

Bridge

Gtr. 3 tacet

*Refers to Gtr. 1 only.

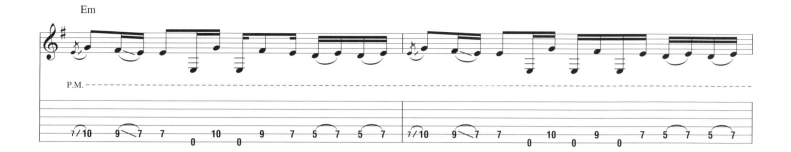

Verse

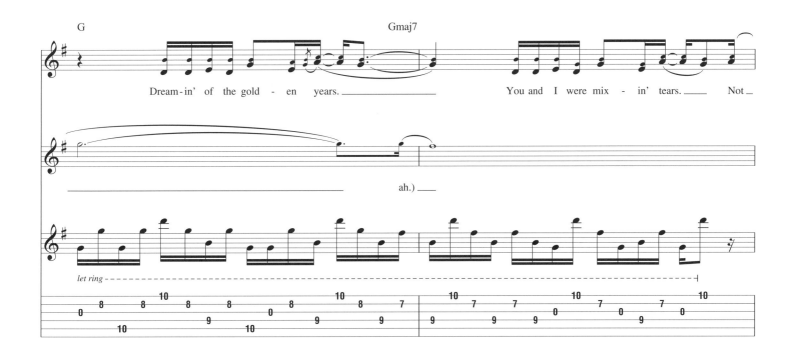

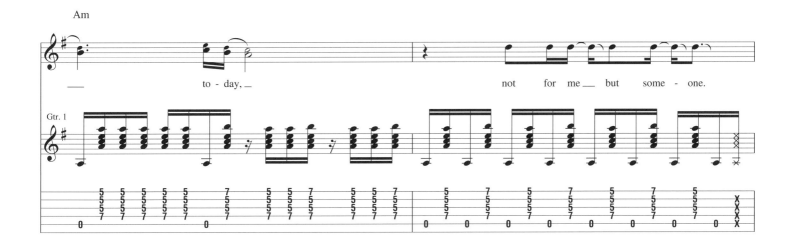

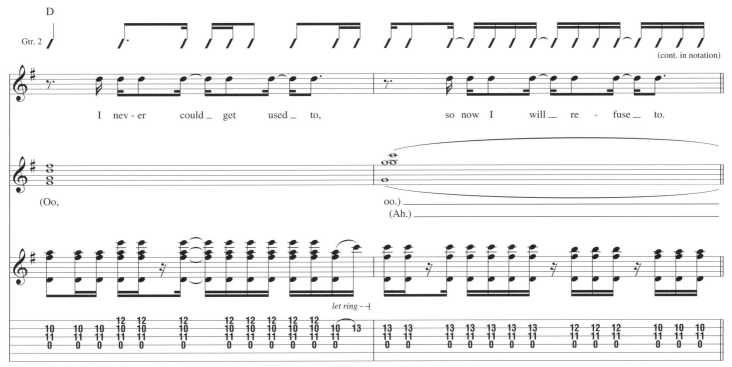

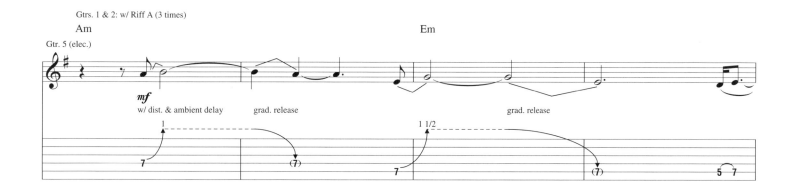

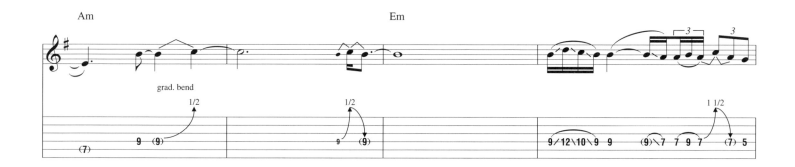

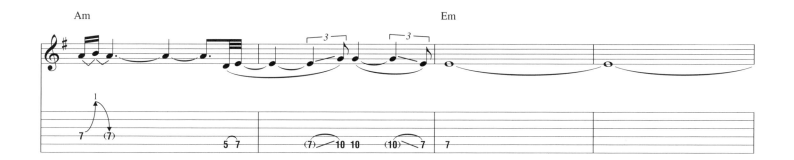

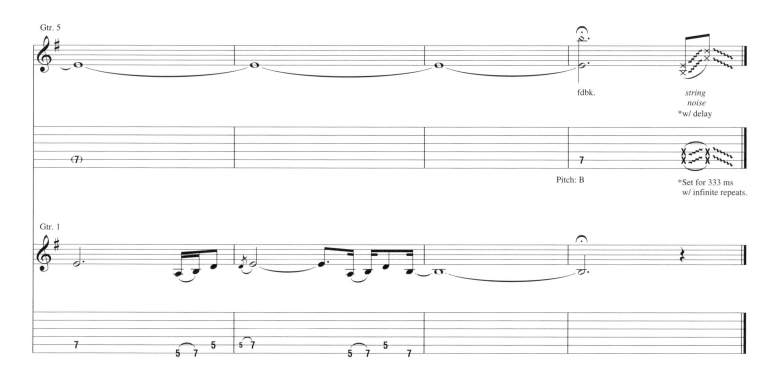

Even You Brutus?

Words and Music by Anthony Kiedis, Flea, Chad Smith and Josh Klinghoffer

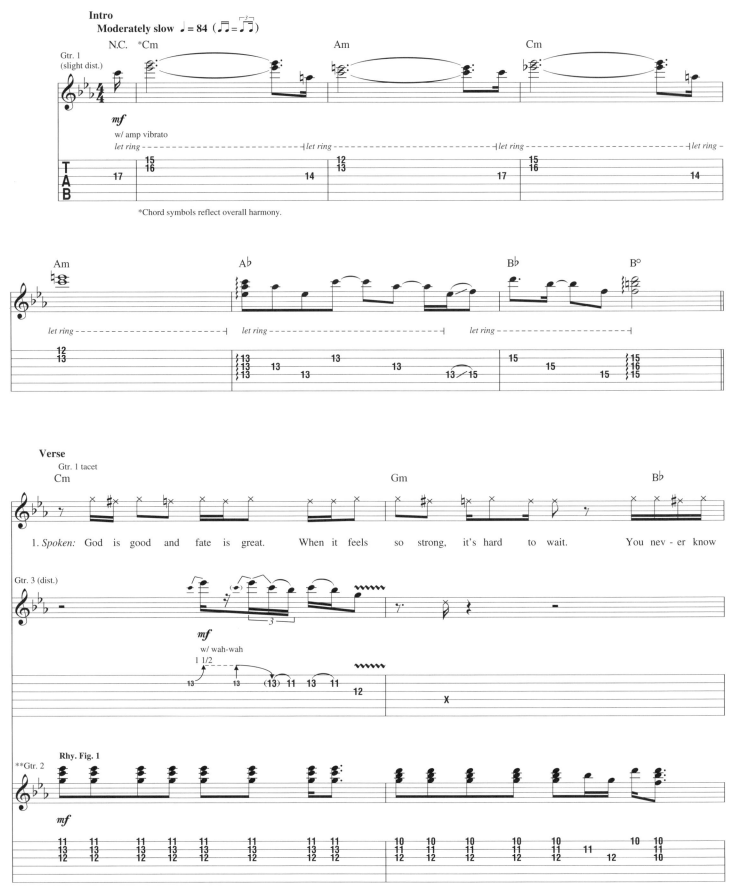

*Chord symbols reflect overall harmony.

**Piano arr. for gtr.

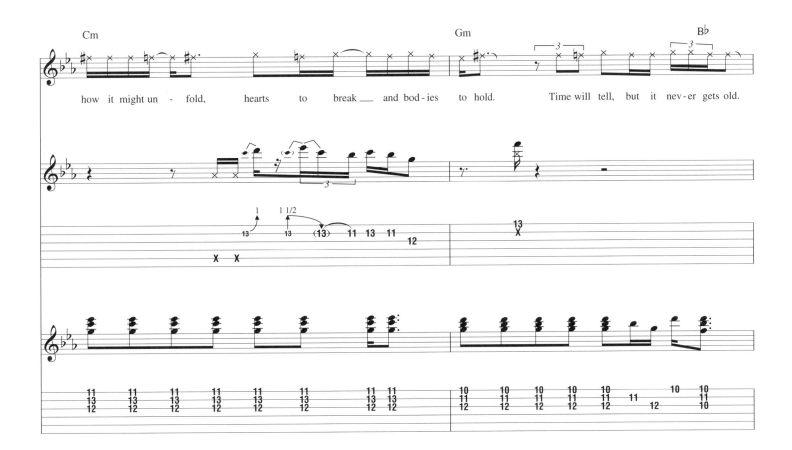

how it might un - fold, hearts to break __ and bod - ies to hold. Time will tell, but it nev - er gets old.

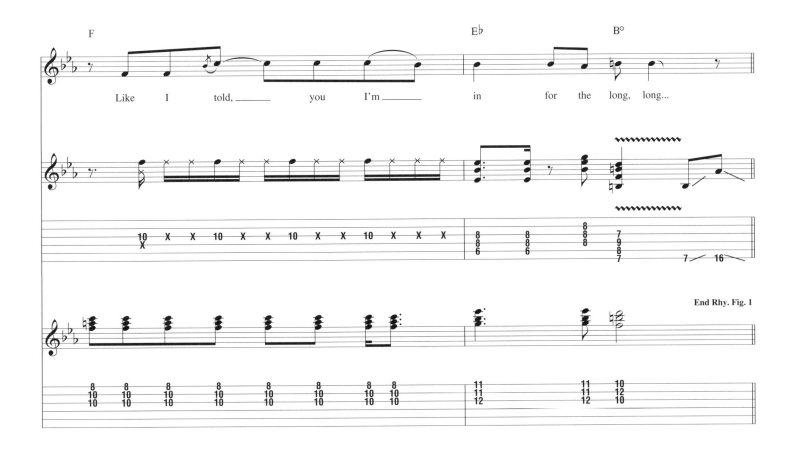

Like I told, _____ you I'm _____ in for the long, long...

End Rhy. Fig. 1

Verse

Gtr. 2: w/ Rhy. Fig. 1 (1st 4 meas.)

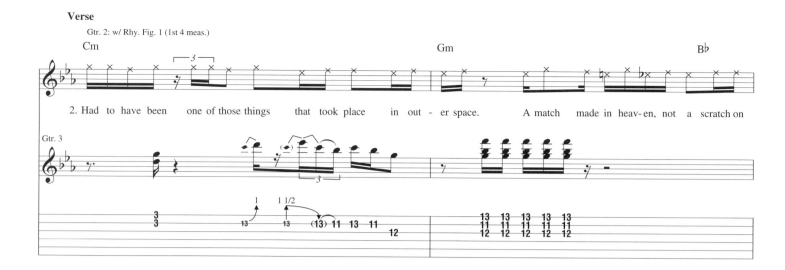

2. Had to have been one of those things that took place in out - er space. A match made in heav - en, not a scratch on

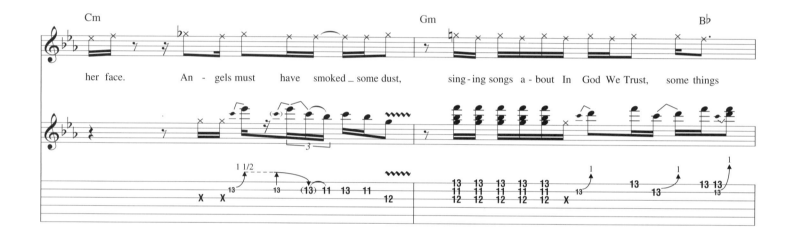

her face. An - gels must have smoked _ some dust, sing - ing songs a - bout In God We Trust, some things

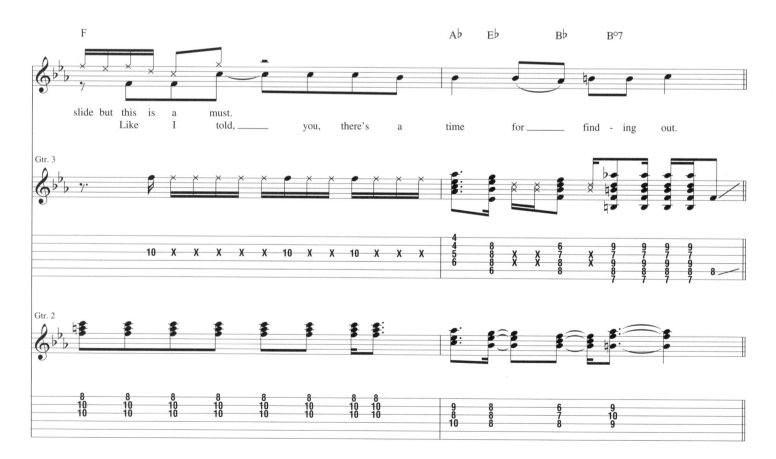

slide but this is a must.
Like I told, _____ you, there's a time for _____ find - ing out.

Verse

Gtr. 2: w/ Rhy. Fig. 1 (1st 4 meas.)

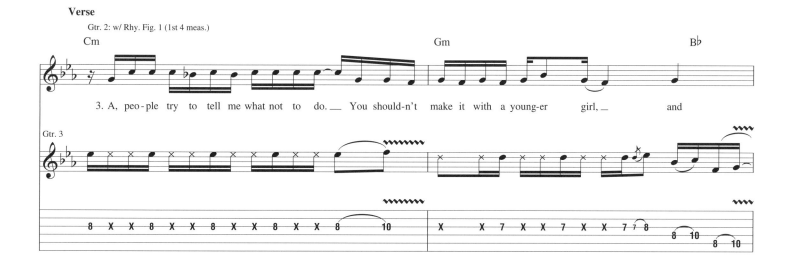

3. A, peo-ple try to tell me what not to do. __ You should-n't make it with a young-er girl, __ and

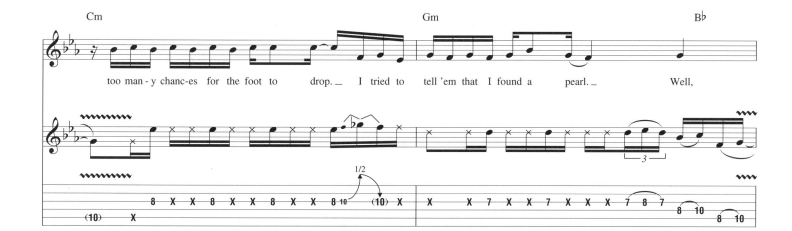

too man-y chanc-es for the foot to drop. __ I tried to tell 'em that I found a pearl. __ Well,

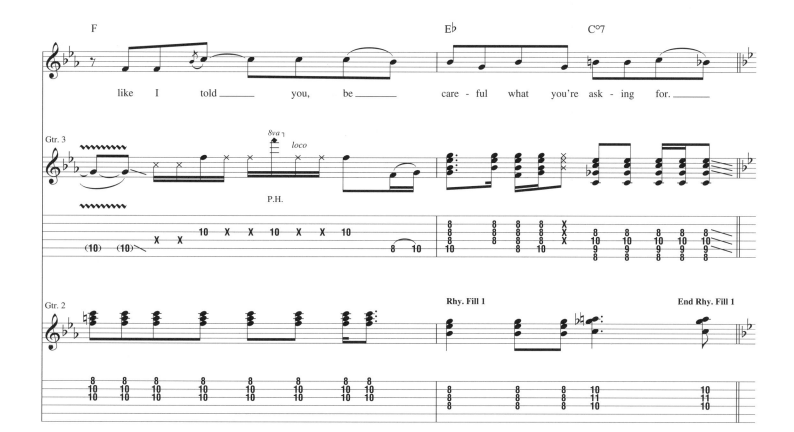

like I told _____ you, be _____ care - ful what you're ask - ing for. _____

Chorus

Hey, sis-ter Bru - tus, got a mess __ of a bet-ter half. __

Aw! Hey, sis-ter Ju - das, e - ven

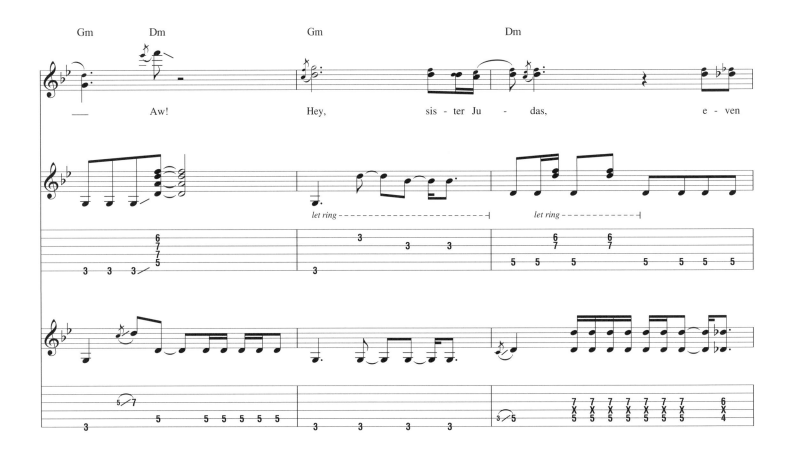

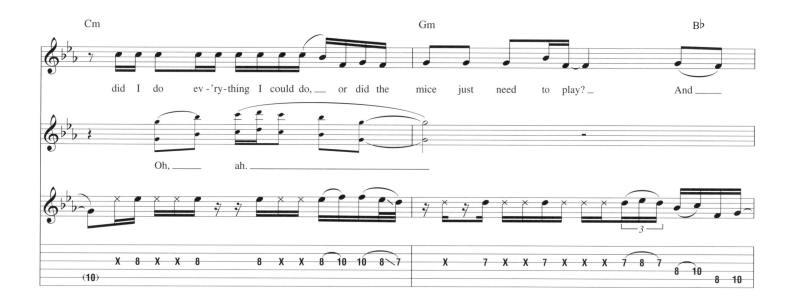

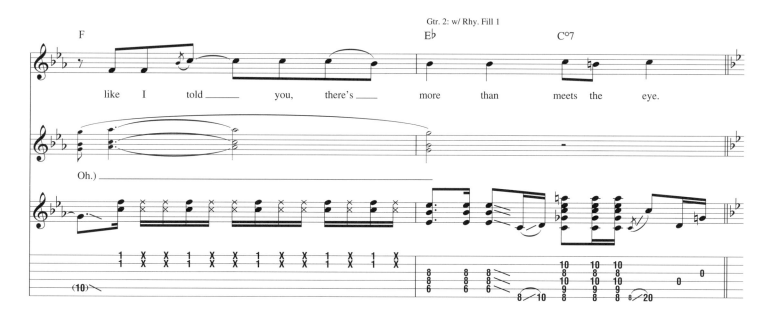

Chorus

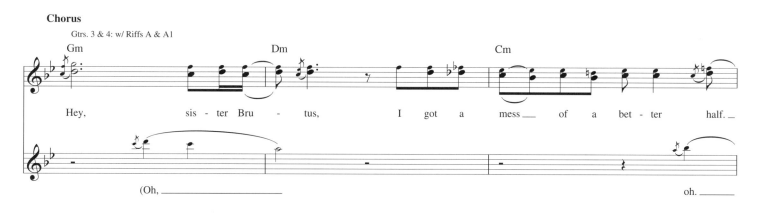

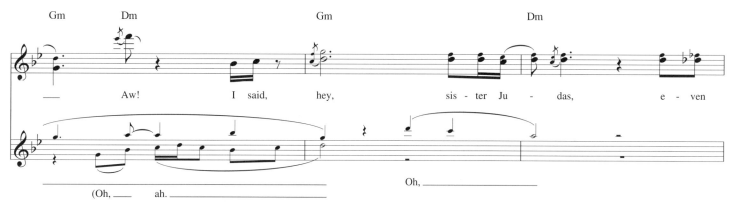

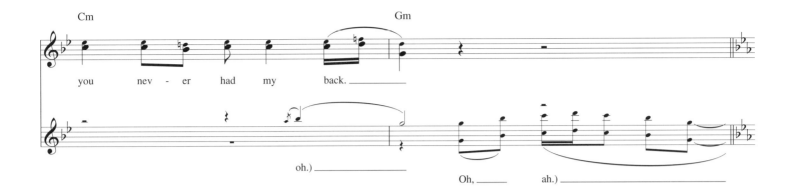

you nev - er had my back. ____

oh.) ____

Oh, ____ ah.)

Bridge

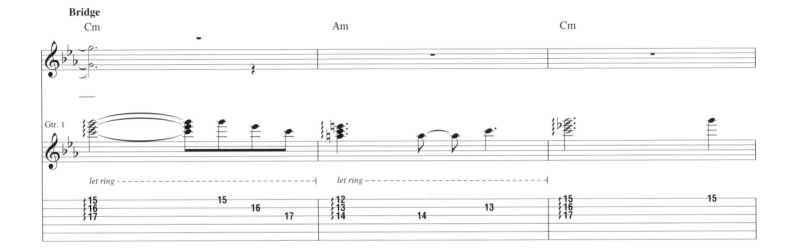

let ring -

let ring -

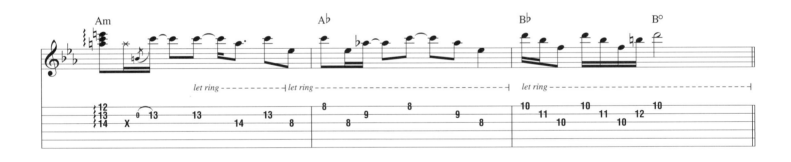

let ring - - - - - - - - | let ring - - - - - - - -

let ring - - - - - - - - - - - - - - - - - -

Verse

Gtr. 1 tacet
Gtr. 2: w/ Rhy. Fig. 1 (1st 5 meas.)

6. I'm not try - in' to point fin - gers at you ___ and I'm not try - in' to lay an - y blame. ____

Gtr. 3

w/ wah-wah

But when it comes to the pun-ish-ment, _ girl, you know how to bring the pain. _____

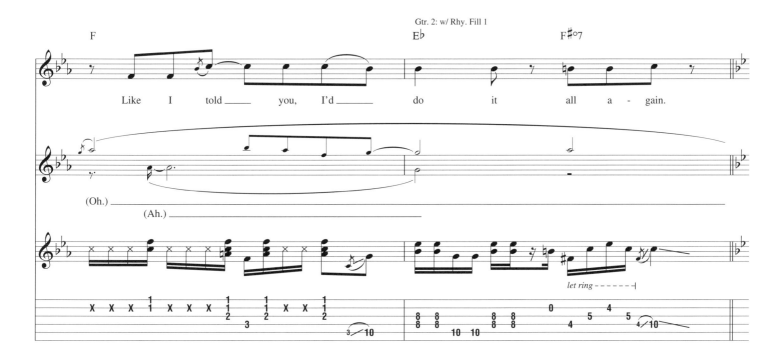

Gtr. 2: w/ Rhy. Fill 1

Like I told _ you, I'd _ do it all a-gain.

(Oh.) ____

(Ah.) ____

let ring - - - - - -

Chorus

Gtrs. 3 & 4: w/ Riffs A & A1 (1 7/8 times)

Hey, sis-ter Bru-tus, I got a mess of a bet-ter half.

____ (Oh, ____ oh. ____

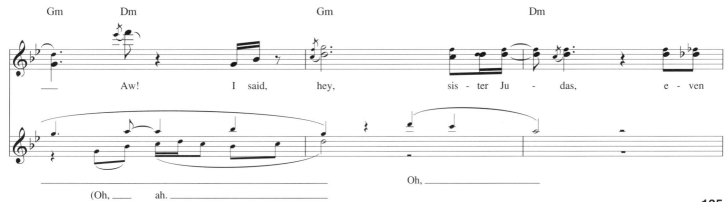

Aw! I said, hey, sis-ter Ju-das, e-ven

(Oh, ____ ah. ____

Oh, ____

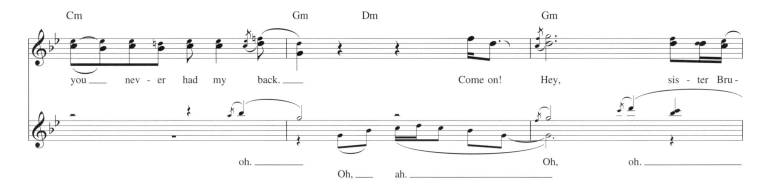

you ___ nev-er had my back. ___ Come on! Hey, sis - ter Bru-

oh. ___ Oh, oh. ___

Oh, ___ ah. ___

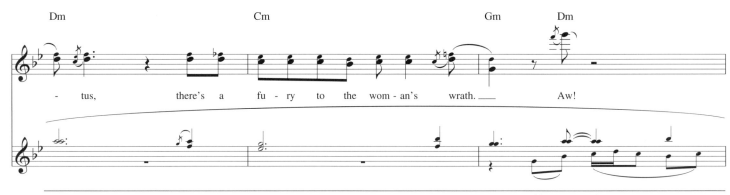

-tus, there's a fu-ry to the wom-an's wrath. ___ Aw!

Oh, ___ ah.) ___

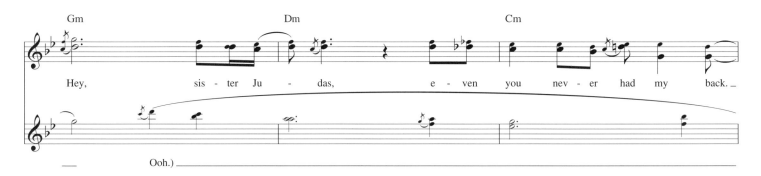

Hey, sis - ter Ju - das, e - ven you nev - er had my back. ___

Ooh.) ___

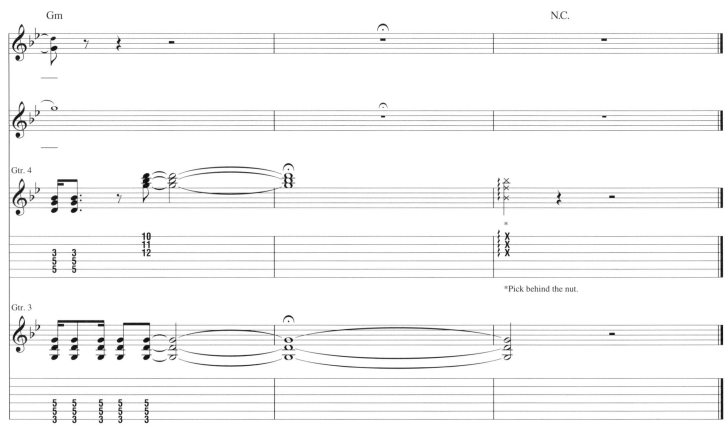

*Pick behind the nut.

Gtr. 3

Meet Me at the Corner

Words and Music by Anthony Kiedis, Flea, Chad Smith and Josh Klinghoffer

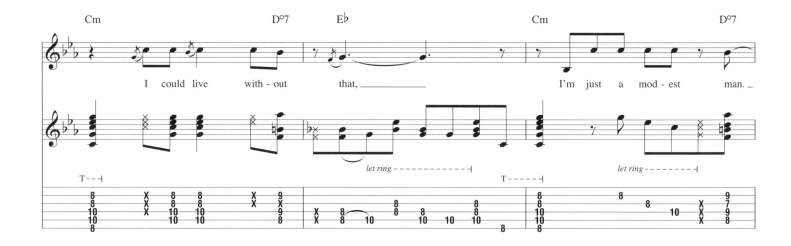

Chorus

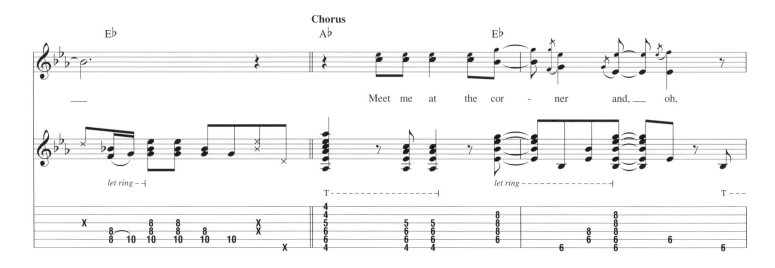

had I known all that I do now, I'm guess - ing we're thru, now.
(Guess - ing we're thru, now.)

Re - ced - ing in - to the for - est, I will lay a - round in wait,

*Bass plays G.

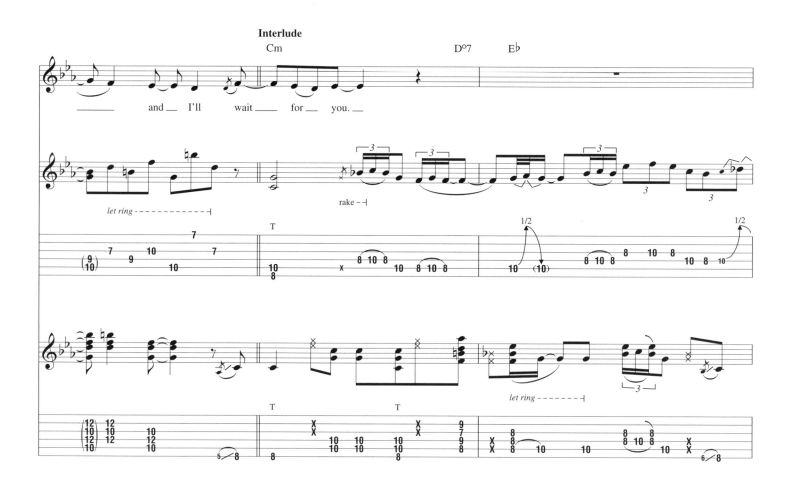

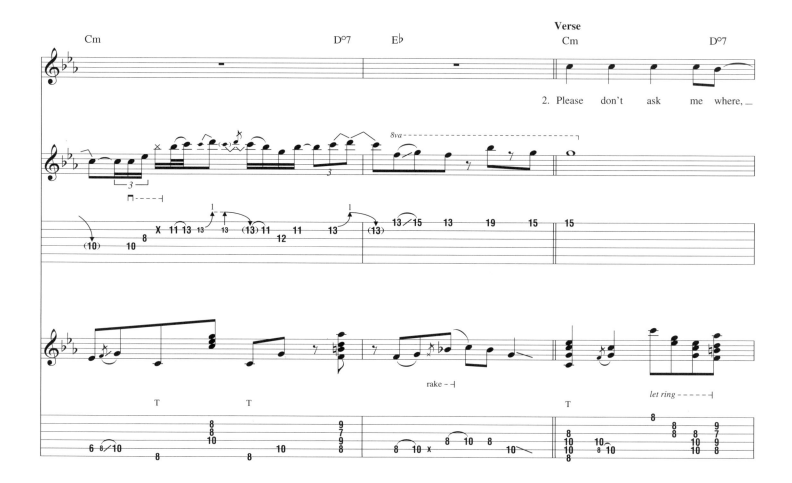

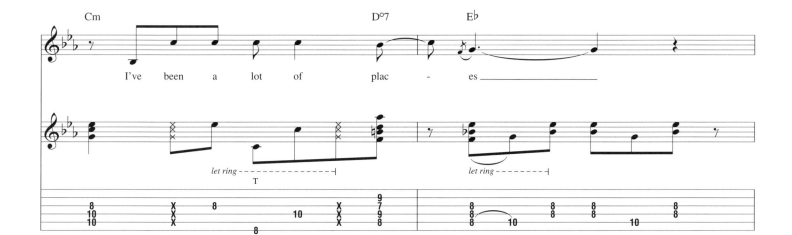

Chorus

had I know all that I do now, I'm guess-ing we're thru, now.
(Guess-ing we're thru, now.)

Re-ced-ing in-to the for-est, I will lay a-round in wait,

and ___ I'll ___ wait ___ for ___ you. ___

Female: I

let ring ----------

let ring ----------

let ring ----------

let ring ----------

Bridge

Gtr. 1 tacet

*Em

Gtr. 3 (elec.)

mf

w/ clean tone

Cmaj7

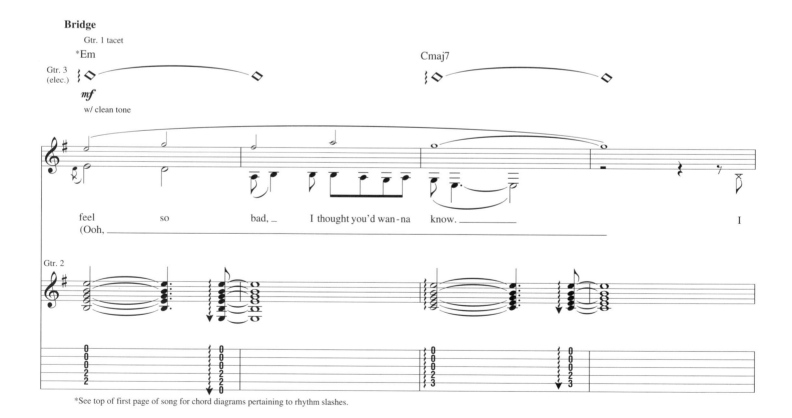

feel ___ so ___ bad, ___ I thought you'd wan-na ___ know. ___

I

(Ooh, ___

Gtr. 2

*See top of first page of song for chord diagrams pertaining to rhythm slashes.

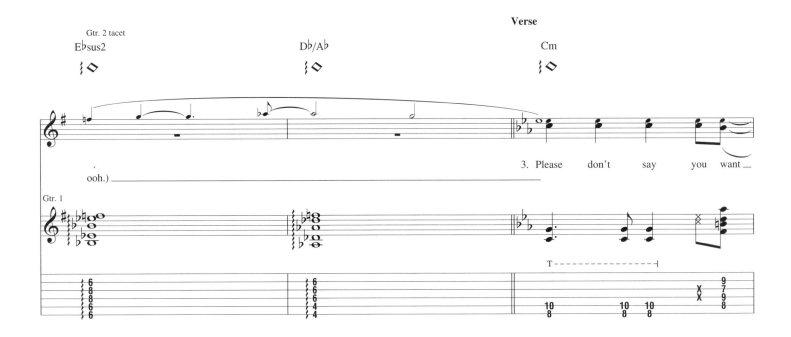

Verse

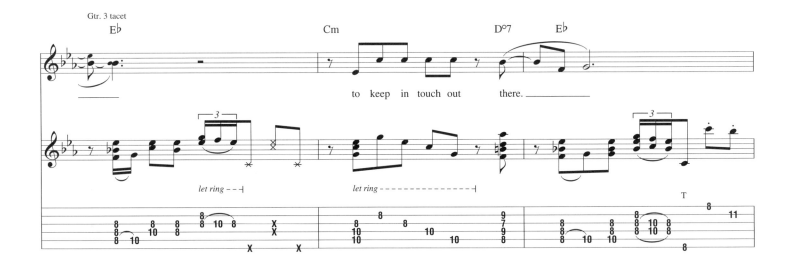

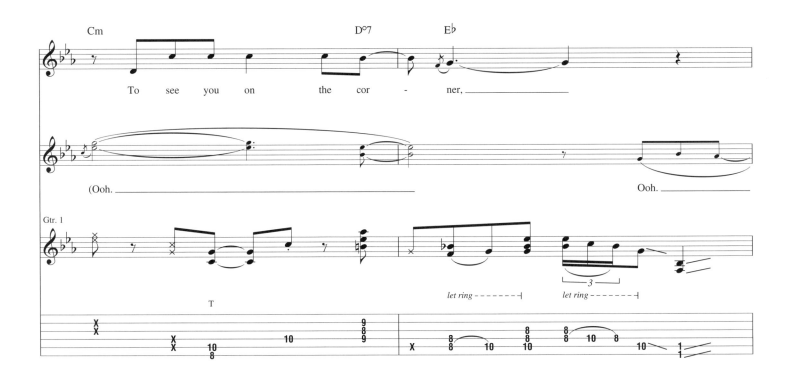

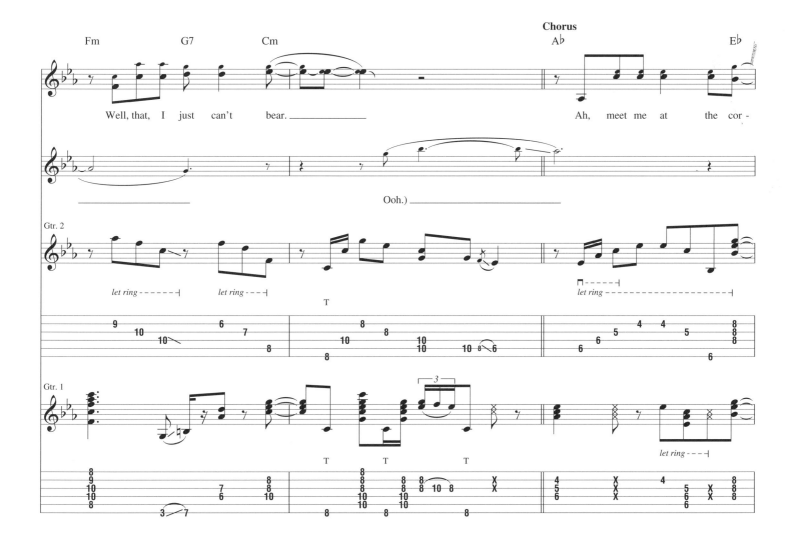

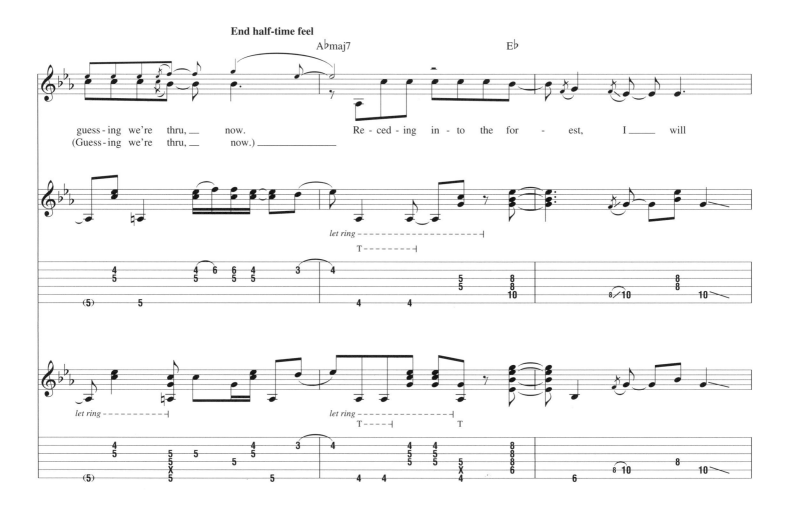

lay a-round in wait.

Bridge

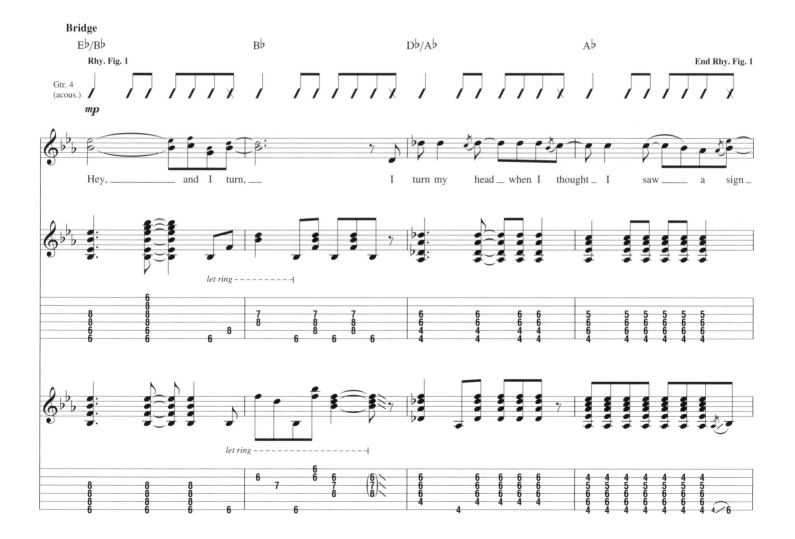

Hey, _____ and I turn, _____ I turn my head _____ when I thought _____ I saw _____ a sign _____

Gtr. 4: w/ Rhy. Fig. 1 (5 times)

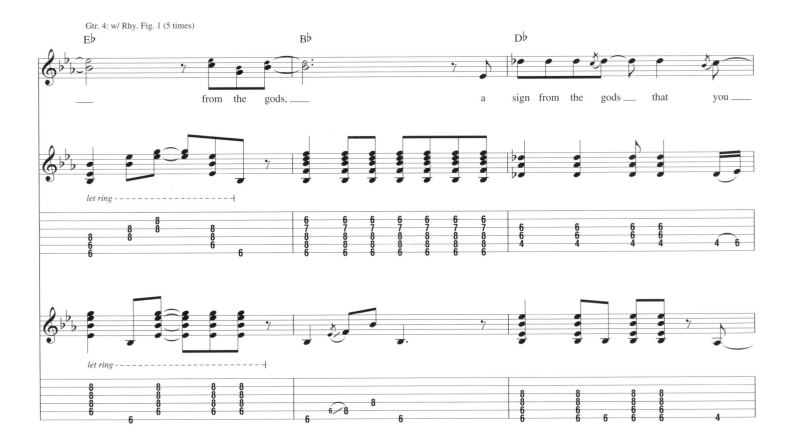

from the gods, ____ a sign from the gods ____ that you ____

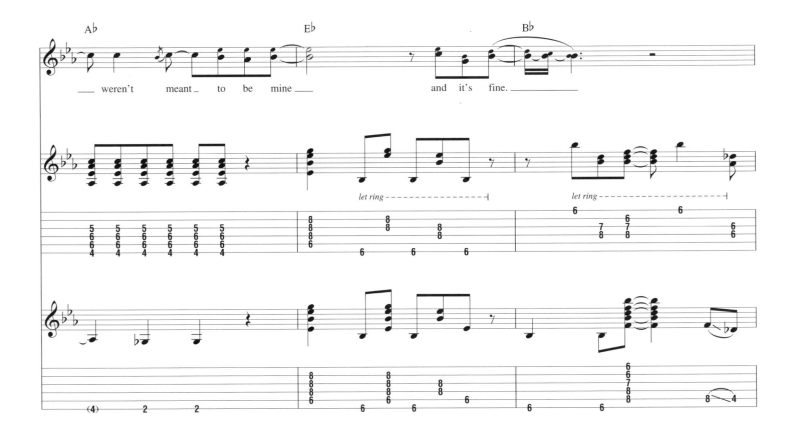

____ weren't meant ____ to be mine ____ and it's fine. ____

150

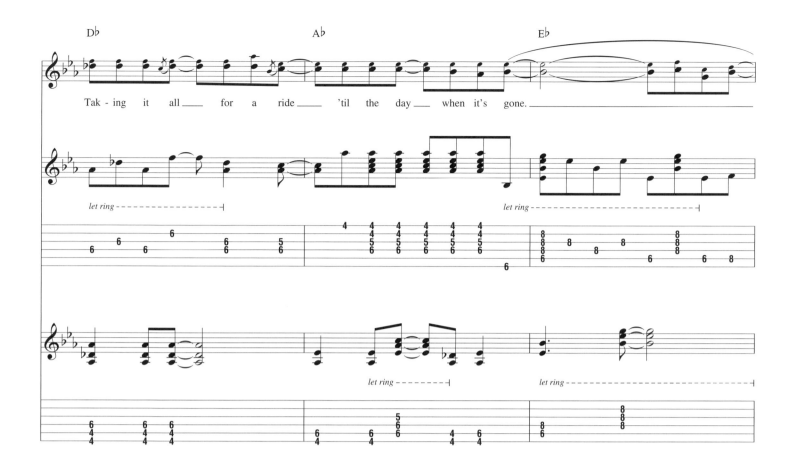

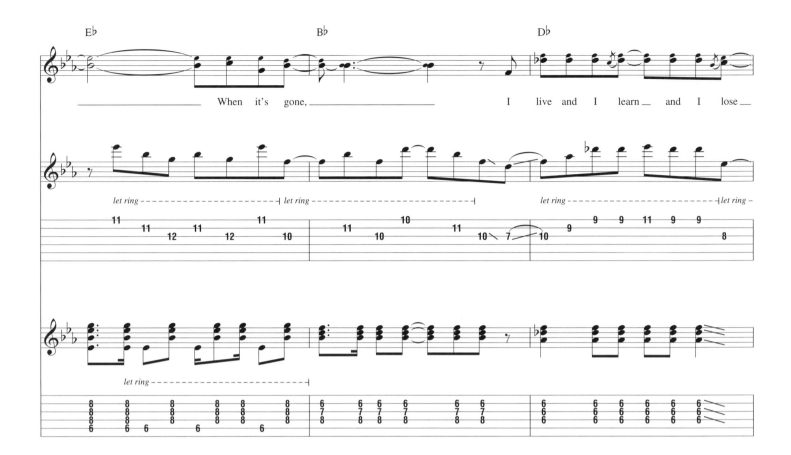

When it's gone,   I live and I learn ___ and I lose ___

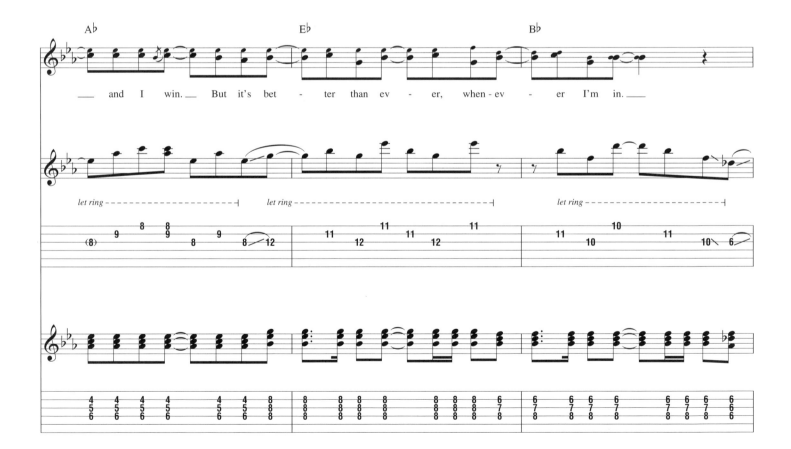

___ and I win. ___ But it's bet - ter than ev - er, when - ev - er I'm in. ___

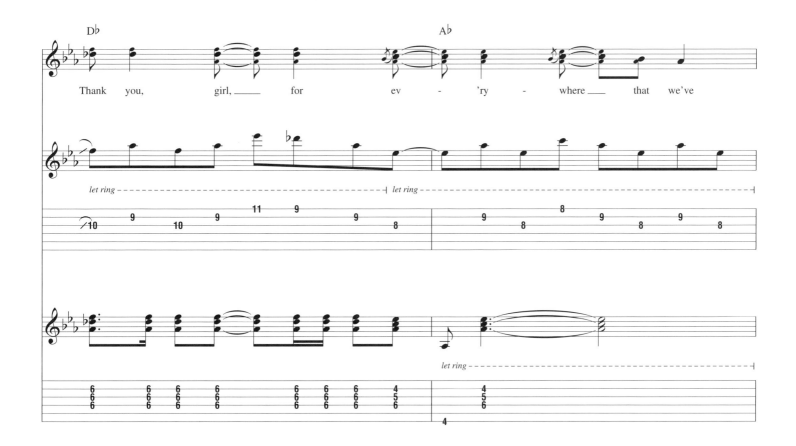

Thank you, girl, ___ for ev - 'ry - where ___ that we've

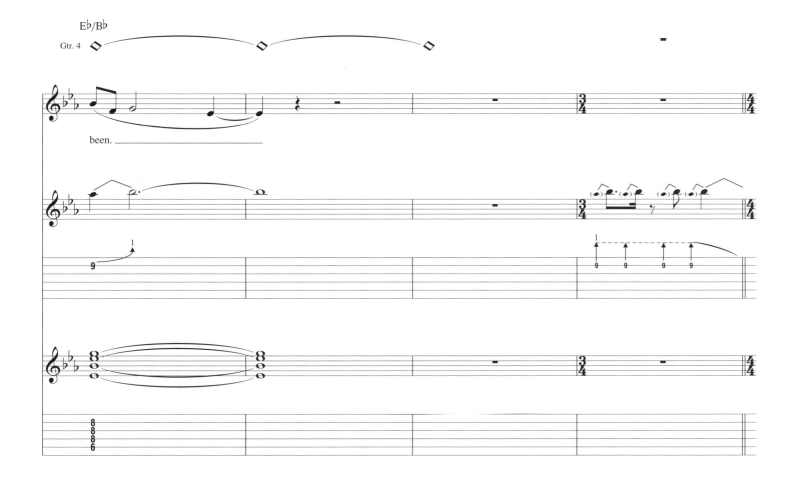

been. ___

Outro

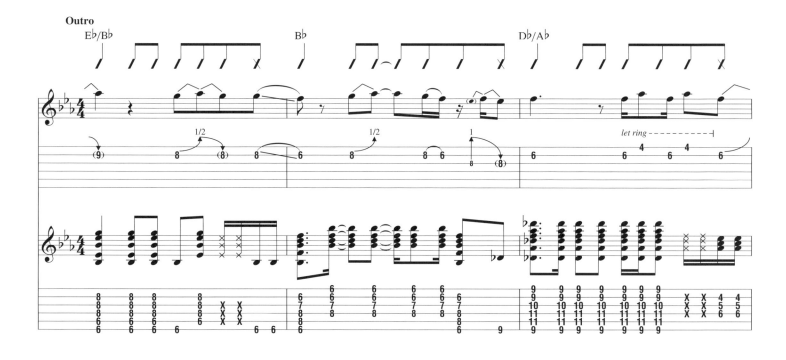

Free time

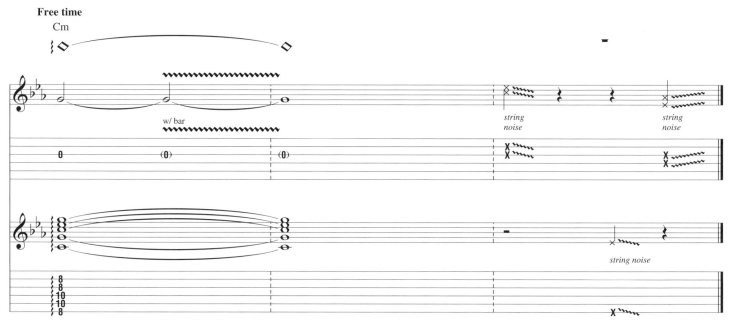

Dance, Dance, Dance

Words and Music by Anthony Kiedis, Flea, Chad Smith and Josh Klinghoffer

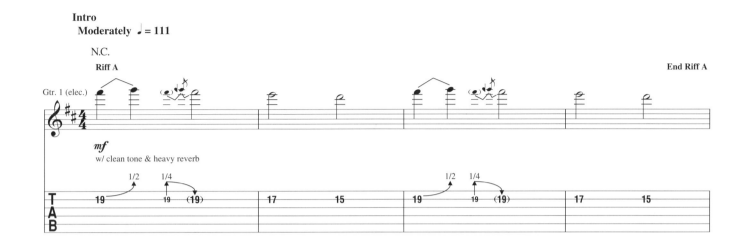

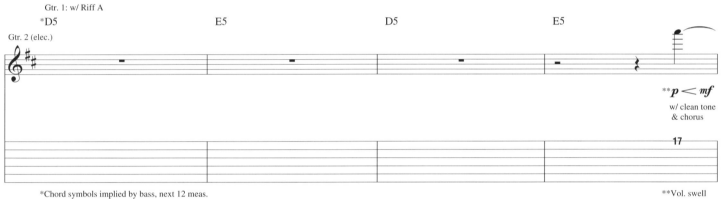

*Chord symbols implied by bass, next 12 meas.

**Vol. swell

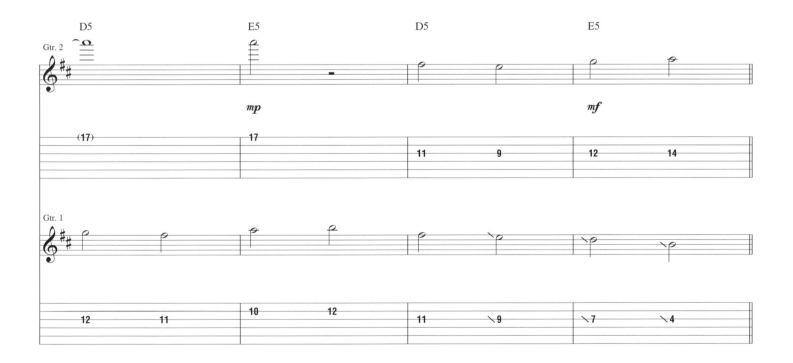

Verse

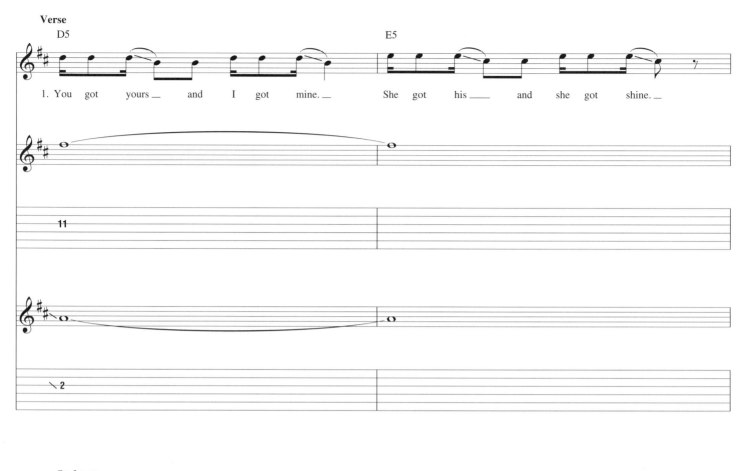

1. You got yours __ and I got mine. She got his __ and she got shine. __

Gtr. 2 tacet

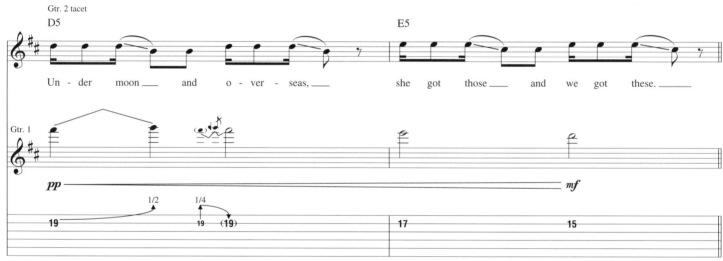

Un-der moon __ and o-ver-seas, __ she got those __ and we got these. _____

pp _____ *mf*

Chorus

Gtr. 1: w/ Riff A (3 3/4 times)

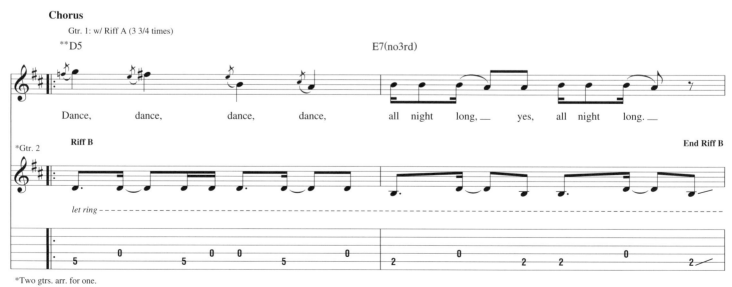

Dance, dance, dance, dance, all night long, __ yes, all night long. __

Gtr. 2 — Riff B — End Riff B

let ring -

*Two gtrs. arr. for one.

**Chord symbols reflect overall harmony.

156

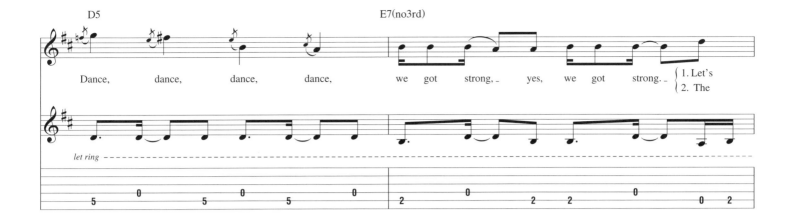

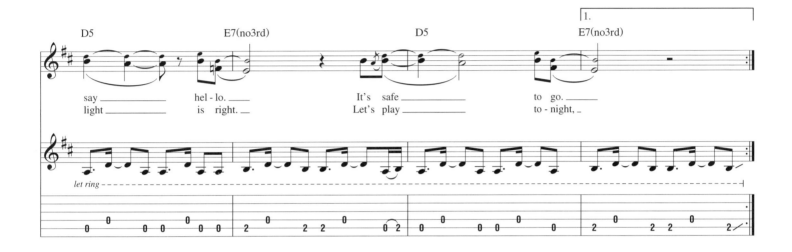

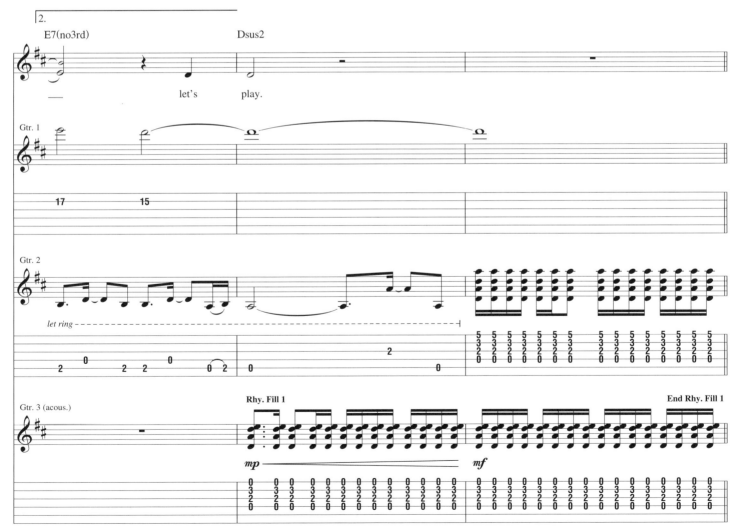

§ Bridge

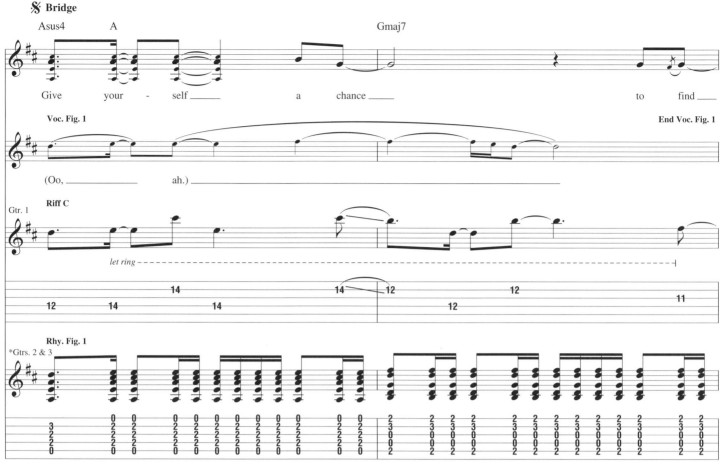

*Composite arrangement

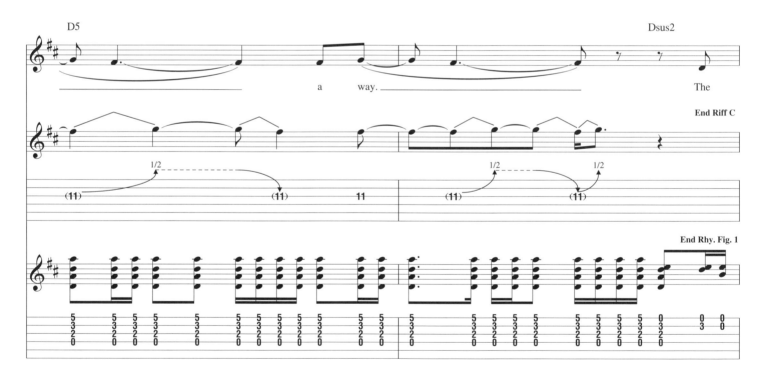

Bkgd. Voc.: w/ Voc. Fig. 1
1st time, Gtr. 1: w/ Riff C
1st time, Gtrs. 2 & 3: w/ Rhy. Fig. 1
2nd time, Gtr. 1: w/ Riff C (3 times)
2nd time, Gtr. 2: w/ Rhy. Fig. 1 (2 times)
2nd time, Gtr. 3: w/ Rhy. Fig. 1 (3 times)

To Coda

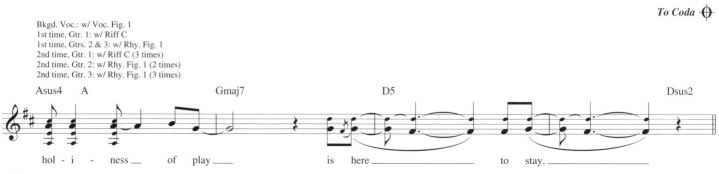

Verse

Gtr. 2: w/ Riff B (2 times)

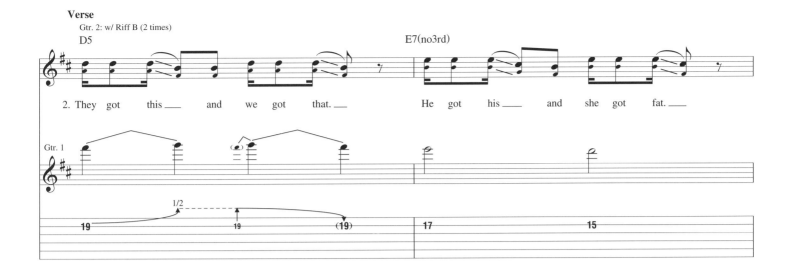

2. They got this ___ and we got that. ___ He got his ___ and she got fat. ___

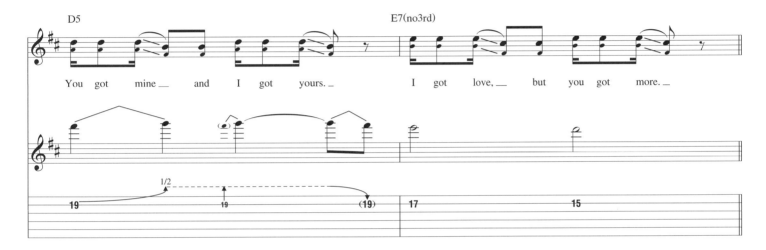

You got mine ___ and I got yours. ___ I got love, ___ but you got more. ___

Chorus

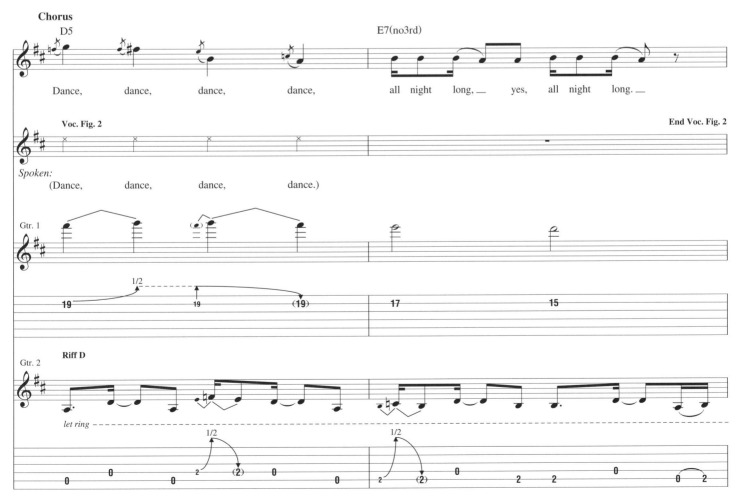

Dance, dance, dance, dance, all night long, ___ yes, all night long. ___

Spoken:
(Dance, dance, dance, dance.)

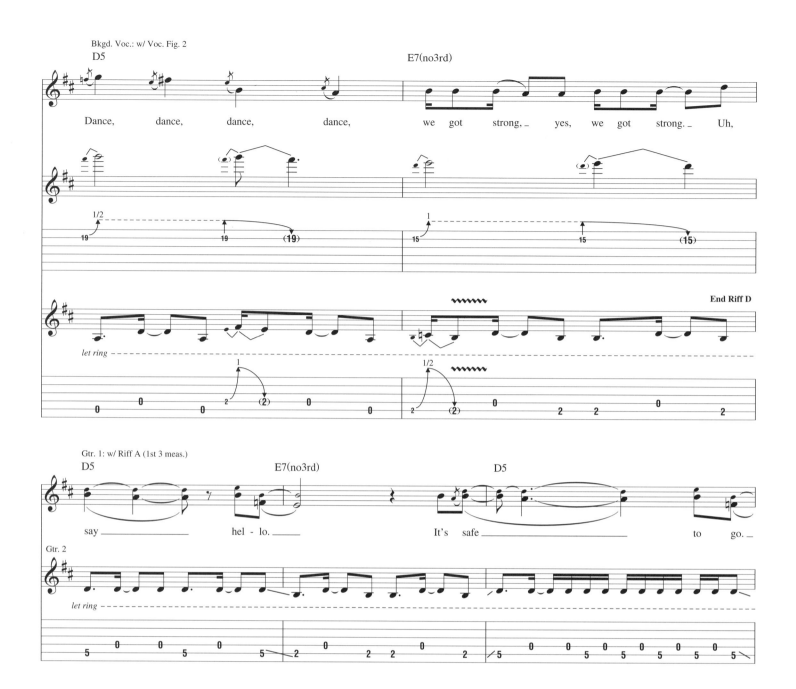

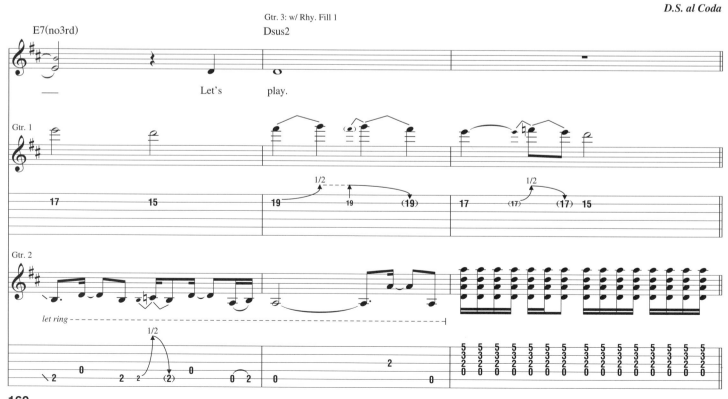

⊕ Coda

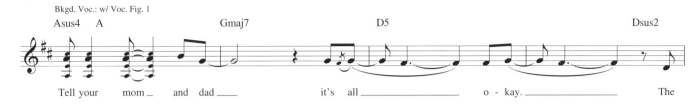

Bkgd. Voc.: w/ Voc. Fig. 1

Asus4 A   Gmaj7   D5   Dsus2

Tell your mom and dad ___ it's all ___ o - kay. ___ The

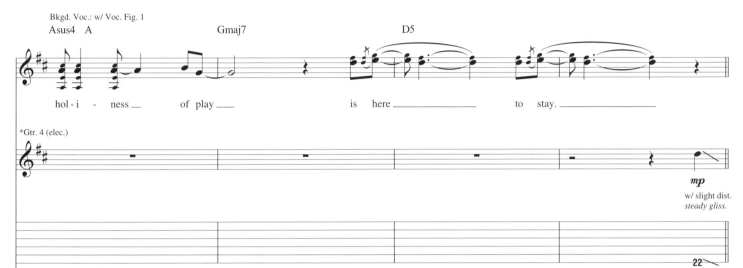

Bkgd. Voc.: w/ Voc. Fig. 1

Asus4 A   Gmaj7   D5

hol - i - ness ___ of play ___ is here ___ to stay. ___

*Gtr. 4 (elec.)

mp
w/ slight dist.
steady gliss.

*Two gtrs. arr. for one.

Gtr. 2

Interlude

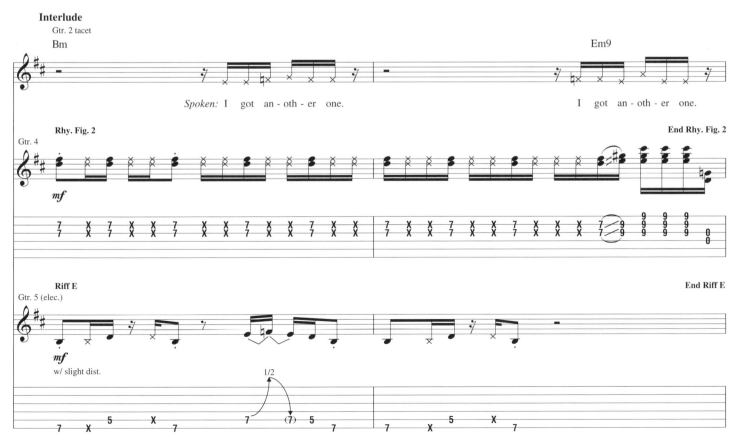

Gtr. 2 tacet

Bm   Em9

Spoken: I got an - oth - er one.   I got an - oth - er one.

Rhy. Fig. 2   **End Rhy. Fig. 2**

Gtr. 4

mf

Riff E   **End Riff E**

Gtr. 5 (elec.)

mf
w/ slight dist.

Gtr. 4: w/ Rhy. Fig. 2 (2 times)
Gtr. 5: w/ Riff E (3 times)

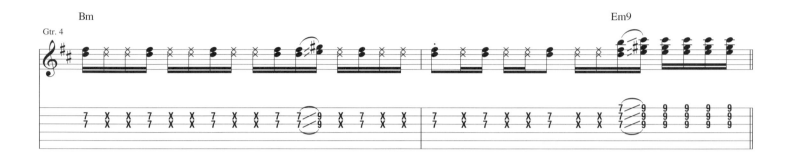

Sung: I got a fun-ny one.　　*Spoken:* I got an-oth-er one.　　*Sung:* Whoa. __　　*Spoken:* I got a sec-ond one.

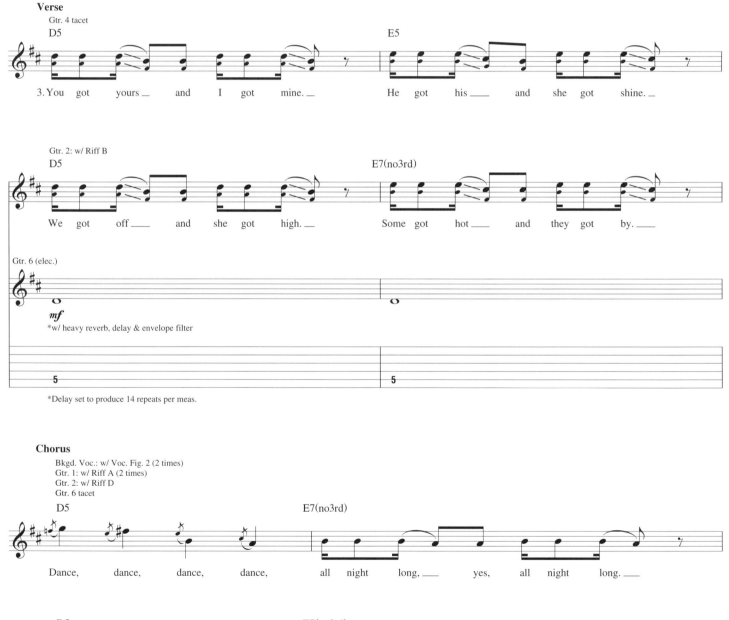

Verse

Gtr. 4 tacet

3. You got yours __ and I got mine. __　　He got his __ and she got shine. __

Gtr. 2: w/ Riff B

We got off __ and she got high. __　　Some got hot __ and they got by. __

Gtr. 6 (elec.)

mf

*w/ heavy reverb, delay & envelope filter

*Delay set to produce 14 repeats per meas.

Chorus

Bkgd. Voc.: w/ Voc. Fig. 2 (2 times)
Gtr. 1: w/ Riff A (2 times)
Gtr. 2: w/ Riff D
Gtr. 6 tacet

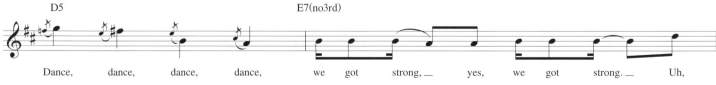

Dance, dance, dance, dance, all night long, __ yes, all night long. __

Dance, dance, dance, dance, we got strong, __ yes, we got strong. __ Uh,

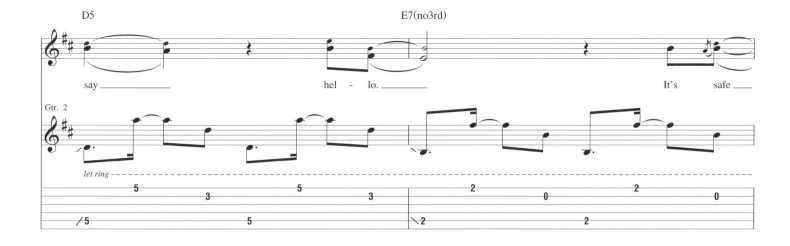

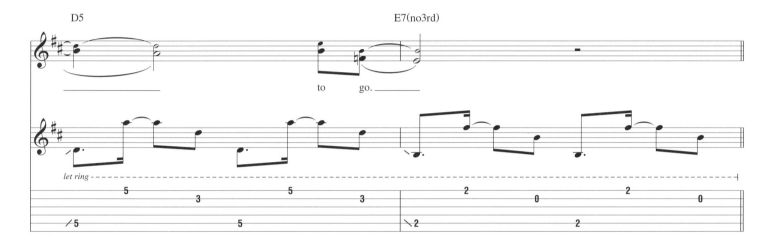

Outro-Chorus

Bkgd. Voc.: w/ Voc. Fig. 1 (2 times)
1st time, Gtr. 1: w/ Riff A (3 times)

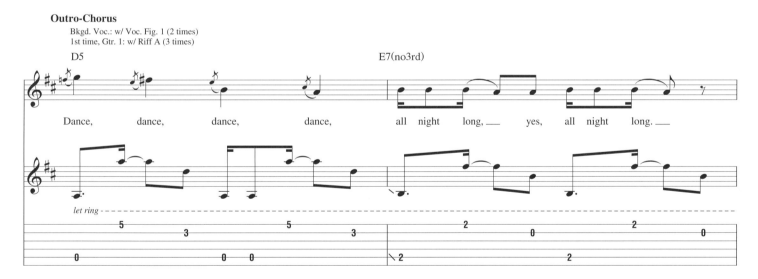

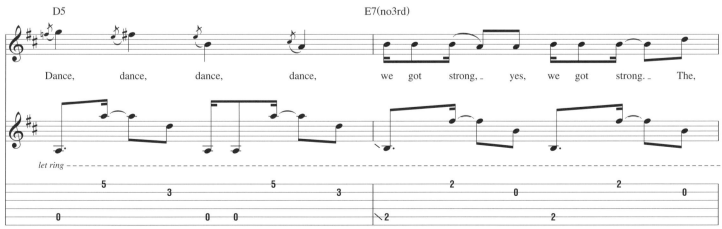

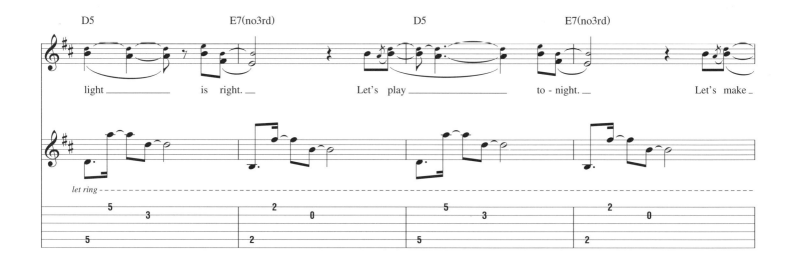

light _____ is right. _____ Let's play _____ to - night. _____ Let's make _

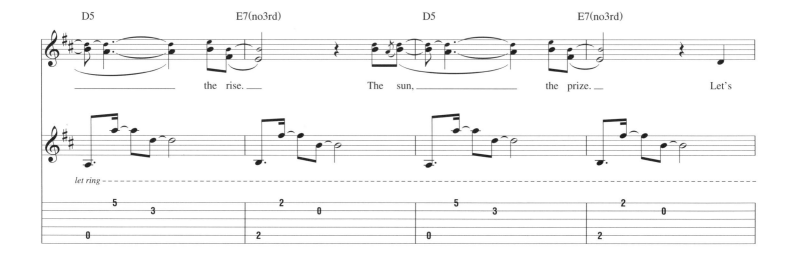

_____ the rise. _____ The sun, _____ the prize. _____ Let's

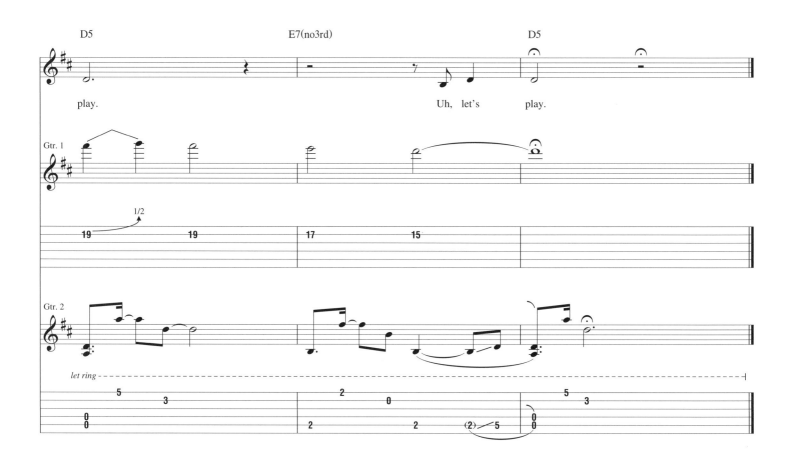

play. Uh, let's play.

GUITAR NOTATION LEGEND

Guitar music can be notated three different ways: on a *musical staff*, in *tablature*, and in *rhythm slashes*.

RHYTHM SLASHES are written above the staff. Strum chords in the rhythm indicated. Use the chord diagrams found at the top of the first page of the transcription for the appropriate chord voicings. Round noteheads indicate single notes.

THE MUSICAL STAFF shows pitches and rhythms and is divided by bar lines into measures. Pitches are named after the first seven letters of the alphabet.

TABLATURE graphically represents the guitar fingerboard. Each horizontal line represents a string, and each number represents a fret.

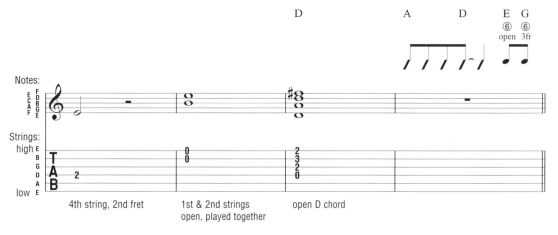

4th string, 2nd fret   1st & 2nd strings open, played together   open D chord

Definitions for Special Guitar Notation

HALF-STEP BEND: Strike the note and bend up 1/2 step.

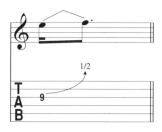

WHOLE-STEP BEND: Strike the note and bend up one step.

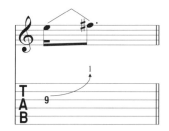

GRACE NOTE BEND: Strike the note and immediately bend up as indicated.

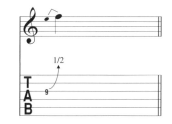

SLIGHT (MICROTONE) BEND: Strike the note and bend up 1/4 step.

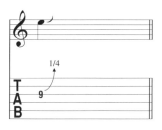

BEND AND RELEASE: Strike the note and bend up as indicated, then release back to the original note. Only the first note is struck.

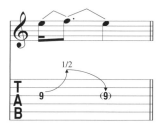

PRE-BEND: Bend the note as indicated, then strike it.

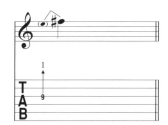

PRE-BEND AND RELEASE: Bend the note as indicated. Strike it and release the bend back to the original note.

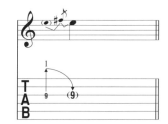

UNISON BEND: Strike the two notes simultaneously and bend the lower note up to the pitch of the higher.

VIBRATO: The string is vibrated by rapidly bending and releasing the note with the fretting hand.

WIDE VIBRATO: The pitch is varied to a greater degree by vibrating with the fretting hand.

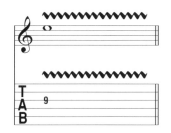

HAMMER-ON: Strike the first (lower) note with one finger, then sound the higher note (on the same string) with another finger by fretting it without picking.

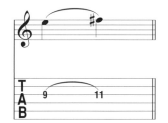

PULL-OFF: Place both fingers on the notes to be sounded. Strike the first note and without picking, pull the finger off to sound the second (lower) note.

LEGATO SLIDE: Strike the first note and then slide the same fret-hand finger up or down to the second note. The second note is not struck.

SHIFT SLIDE: Same as legato slide, except the second note is struck.

TRILL: Very rapidly alternate between the notes indicated by continuously hammering on and pulling off.

TAPPING: Hammer ("tap") the fret indicated with the pick-hand index or middle finger and pull off to the note fretted by the fret hand.

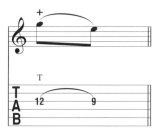

NATURAL HARMONIC: Strike the note while the fret-hand lightly touches the string directly over the fret indicated.

Harm.

PINCH HARMONIC: The note is fretted normally and a harmonic is produced by adding the edge of the thumb or the tip of the index finger of the pick hand to the normal pick attack.

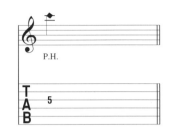

P.H.

HARP HARMONIC: The note is fretted normally and a harmonic is produced by gently resting the pick hand's index finger directly above the indicated fret (in parentheses) while the pick hand's thumb or pick assists by plucking the appropriate string.

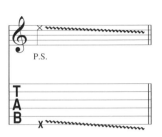

H.H.

PICK SCRAPE: The edge of the pick is rubbed down (or up) the string, producing a scratchy sound.

P.S.

MUFFLED STRINGS: A percussive sound is produced by laying the fret hand across the string(s) without depressing, and striking them with the pick hand.

PALM MUTING: The note is partially muted by the pick hand lightly touching the string(s) just before the bridge.

P.M.

RAKE: Drag the pick across the strings indicated with a single motion.

rake - - -

TREMOLO PICKING: The note is picked as rapidly and continuously as possible.

ARPEGGIATE: Play the notes of the chord indicated by quickly rolling them from bottom to top.

VIBRATO BAR DIVE AND RETURN: The pitch of the note or chord is dropped a specified number of steps (in rhythm), then returned to the original pitch.

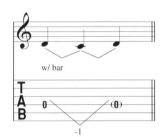

w/ bar

VIBRATO BAR SCOOP: Depress the bar just before striking the note, then quickly release the bar.

w/ bar - - - - - - - - -

VIBRATO BAR DIP: Strike the note and then immediately drop a specified number of steps, then release back to the original pitch.

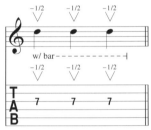

w/ bar - - - - - - - - -

Additional Musical Definitions

(accent)	• Accentuate note (play it louder).	

(accent)	• Accentuate note with great intensity.	

(staccato)	• Play the note short.	

⊓ • Downstroke

∨ • Upstroke

D.S. al Coda • Go back to the sign (𝄋), then play until the measure marked "***To Coda***," then skip to the section labelled "**Coda**."

D.C. al Fine • Go back to the beginning of the song and play until the measure marked "***Fine***" (end).

Rhy. Fig. • Label used to recall a recurring accompaniment pattern (usually chordal).

Riff • Label used to recall composed, melodic lines (usually single notes) which recur.

Fill • Label used to identify a brief melodic figure which is to be inserted into the arrangement.

Rhy. Fill • A chordal version of a Fill.

tacet • Instrument is silent (drops out).

• Repeat measures between signs.

| 1. | 2. | • When a repeated section has different endings, play the first ending only the first time and the second ending only the second time. |

NOTE: Tablature numbers in parentheses mean:
    1. The note is being sustained over a system (note in standard notation is tied), or
    2. The note is sustained, but a new articulation (such as a hammer-on, pull-off, slide or vibrato) begins, or
    3. The note is a barely audible "ghost" note (note in standard notation is also in parentheses).

GUITAR RECORDED VERSIONS®

Guitar Recorded Versions® are note-for-note transcriptions of guitar music taken directly off recordings. This series, one of the most popular in print today, features some of the greatest guitar players and groups from blues and rock to country and jazz.

Guitar Recorded Versions are transcribed by the best transcribers in the business. Every book contains notes and tablature. Visit www.halleonard.com for our complete selection.

00690814	John 5 Songs for Sanity	$19.95
00690751	John 5 – Vertigo	$19.95
00694912	Eric Johnson – Ah Via Musicom	$19.95
00690660	Best of Eric Johnson	$19.95
00690845	Eric Johnson – Bloom	$19.95
00690169	Eric Johnson – Venus Isle	$22.95
00690846	Jack Johnson and Friends – Sing-A-Longs and Lullabies for the Film Curious George	$19.95
00690271	Robert Johnson – The New Transcriptions	$24.95
00699131	Best of Janis Joplin	$19.95
00690427	Best of Judas Priest	$22.99
00690651	Juanes – Exitos de Juanes	$19.95
00690277	Best of Kansas	$19.95
00690911	Best of Phil Keaggy	$24.99
00690727	Toby Keith Guitar Collection	$19.95
00690742	The Killers – Hot Fuss	$19.95
00690888	The Killers – Sam's Town	$19.95
00690504	Very Best of Albert King	$19.95
00690444	B.B. King & Eric Clapton – Riding with the King	$19.95
00691134	Freddie King Collection	$19.95
00691062	Kings of Leon – Come Around Sundown	$22.99
00690975	Kings of Leon – Only by the Night	$22.99
00690339	Best of the Kinks	$19.95
00690157	Kiss – Alive!	$19.95
00690356	Kiss – Alive II	$22.99
00694903	Best of Kiss for Guitar	$24.95
00690355	Kiss – Destroyer	$16.95
14026320	Mark Knopfler – Get Lucky	$22.99
00690164	Mark Knopfler Guitar – Vol. 1	$19.95
00690163	Mark Knopfler/Chet Atkins – Neck and Neck	$19.95
00690780	Korn – Greatest Hits, Volume 1	$22.95
00690836	Korn – See You on the Other Side	$19.95
00690377	Kris Kristofferson Collection	$19.95
00690861	Kutless – Hearts of the Innocent	$19.95
00690834	Lamb of God – Ashes of the Wake	$19.95
00690875	Lamb of God – Sacrament	$19.95
00690977	Ray LaMontagne – Gossip in the Grain	$19.99
00690890	Ray LaMontagne – Till the Sun Turns Black	$19.95
00690823	Ray LaMontagne – Trouble	$19.95
00691057	Ray LaMontagne and the Pariah Dogs – God Willin' & The Creek Don't Rise	$22.99
00690658	Johnny Lang – Long Time Coming	$19.95
00690726	Avril Lavigne – Under My Skin	$19.95
00690679	John Lennon – Guitar Collection	$19.95
00690781	Linkin Park – Hybrid Theory	$22.95
00690782	Linkin Park – Meteora	$22.95
00690922	Linkin Park – Minutes to Midnight	$19.95
00690783	Best of Live	$19.95
00699623	The Best of Chuck Loeb	$19.95
00690743	Los Lonely Boys	$19.95
00690720	Lostprophets – Start Something	$19.95
00690525	Best of George Lynch	$24.99
00690955	Lynyrd Skynyrd – All-Time Greatest Hits	$19.99
00694954	New Best of Lynyrd Skynyrd	$19.95
00690577	Yngwie Malmsteen – Anthology	$24.95
00694845	Yngwie Malmsteen – Fire and Ice	$19.95
00694755	Yngwie Malmsteen's Rising Force	$19.95
00694757	Yngwie Malmsteen – Trilogy	$19.95
00690754	Marilyn Manson – Lest We Forget	$19.95
00694956	Bob Marley – Legend	$19.95
00690548	Very Best of Bob Marley & The Wailers – One Love	$22.99
00694945	Bob Marley – Songs of Freedom	$24.95
00690914	Maroon 5 – It Won't Be Soon Before Long	$19.95
00690657	Maroon 5 – Songs About Jane	$19.95
00690748	Maroon 5 – 1.22.03 Acoustic	$19.95
00690989	Mastodon – Crack the Skye	$22.99
00690442	Matchbox 20 – Mad Season	$19.95
00690616	Matchbox Twenty – More Than You Think You Are	$19.95
00690239	Matchbox 20 – Yourself or Someone like You	$19.95
00691034	Andy McKee – Joyland	$19.99
00690382	Sarah McLachlan – Mirrorball	$19.95
00120080	The Don McLean Songbook	$19.95
00694952	Megadeth – Countdown to Extinction	$22.95
00690244	Megadeth – Cryptic Writings	$19.95
00694951	Megadeth – Rust in Peace	$22.95
00690011	Megadeth – Youthanasia	$19.95
00690505	John Mellencamp Guitar Collection	$19.95
00690562	Pat Metheny – Bright Size Life	$19.95
00690646	Pat Metheny – One Quiet Night	$19.95
00690559	Pat Metheny – Question & Answer	$19.95
00690040	Steve Miller Band Greatest Hits	$19.95
00690769	Modest Mouse – Good News for People Who Love Bad News	$19.95
00694802	Gary Moore – Still Got the Blues	$22.99
00691005	Best of Motion City Soundtrack	$19.99
00690787	Mudvayne – L.D. 50	$22.95
00690996	My Morning Jacket Collection	$19.99

00690984	Matt Nathanson – Some Mad Hope	$22.99
00690611	Nirvana	$22.95
00694895	Nirvana – Bleach	$19.95
00690189	Nirvana – From the Muddy Banks of the Wishkah	$19.95
00694913	Nirvana – In Utero	$19.95
00694883	Nirvana – Nevermind	$19.95
00690026	Nirvana – Unplugged in New York	$19.95
00120112	No Doubt – Tragic Kingdom	$22.95
00690121	Oasis – (What's the Story) Morning Glory	$19.95
00690226	Oasis – The Other Side of Oasis	$19.95
00690358	The Offspring – Americana	$19.95
00690203	The Offspring – Smash	$18.95
00690818	The Best of Opeth	$22.95
00691052	Roy Orbison – Black & White Night	$22.99
00694847	Best of Ozzy Osbourne	$22.95
00690921	Ozzy Osbourne – Black Rain	$19.95
00690399	Ozzy Osbourne – The Ozzman Cometh	$19.95
00690129	Ozzy Osbourne – Ozzmosis	$22.95
00690933	Best of Brad Paisley	$22.95
00690995	Brad Paisley – Play: The Guitar Album	$24.99
00690866	Panic! At the Disco – A Fever You Can't Sweat Out	$19.95
00690885	Papa Roach – The Paramour Sessions	$19.95
00690939	Christopher Parkening – Solo Pieces	$19.99
00690594	Best of Les Paul	$19.95
00694855	Pearl Jam – Ten	$19.95
00690439	A Perfect Circle – Mer De Noms	$19.95
00690661	A Perfect Circle – Thirteenth Step	$19.95
00690725	Best of Carl Perkins	$19.99
00690499	Tom Petty – Definitive Guitar Collection	$19.95
00690868	Tom Petty – Highway Companion	$19.95
00690176	Phish – Billy Breathes	$22.95
00690428	Pink Floyd – Dark Side of the Moon	$19.95
00690789	Best of Poison	$19.95
00693864	Best of The Police	$19.95
00690299	Best of Elvis: The King of Rock 'n' Roll	$19.95
00692535	Elvis Presley	$19.95
00690003	Classic Queen	$24.95
00694975	Queen – Greatest Hits	$24.95
00690670	Very Best of Queensryche	$19.95
00690878	The Raconteurs – Broken Boy Soldiers	$19.95
00694910	Rage Against the Machine	$19.95
00690179	Rancid – And Out Come the Wolves	$22.95
00690426	Best of Ratt	$19.95
00690055	Red Hot Chili Peppers – Blood Sugar Sex Magik	$19.95
00690584	Red Hot Chili Peppers – By the Way	$19.95
00690379	Red Hot Chili Peppers – Californication	$19.95
00690673	Red Hot Chili Peppers – Greatest Hits	$19.95
00690090	Red Hot Chili Peppers – One Hot Minute	$22.95
00690852	Red Hot Chili Peppers – Stadium Arcadium	$24.95
00690893	The Red Jumpsuit Apparatus – Don't You Fake It	$19.95
00690511	Django Reinhardt – The Definitive Collection	$19.95
00690779	Relient K – MMHMM	$19.95
00690643	Relient K – Two Lefts Don't Make a Right ... But Three Do	$19.95
00694899	R.E.M. – Automatic for the People	$19.95
00690260	Jimmie Rodgers Guitar Collection	$19.95
00690014	Rolling Stones – Exile on Main Street	$24.95
00690631	Rolling Stones – Guitar Anthology	$27.95
00690685	David Lee Roth – Eat 'Em and Smile	$19.95
00690031	Santana's Greatest Hits	$19.95
00690796	Very Best of Michael Schenker	$19.95
00690566	Best of Scorpions	$22.95
00690604	Bob Seger – Guitar Anthology	$19.95
00690659	Bob Seger and the Silver Bullet Band – Greatest Hits, Volume 2	$17.95
00691012	Shadows Fall – Retribution	$22.99
00690896	Shadows Fall – Threads of Life	$19.95
00690803	Best of Kenny Wayne Shepherd Band	$19.95
00690750	Kenny Wayne Shepherd – The Place You're In	$19.95
00690857	Shinedown – Us and Them	$19.95
00690196	Silverchair – Freak Show	$19.95
00690130	Silverchair – Frogstomp	$19.95
00690872	Slayer – Christ Illusion	$19.95
00690813	Slayer – Guitar Collection	$19.95
00690419	Slipknot	$19.95
00690973	Slipknot – All Hope Is Gone	$22.99
00690733	Slipknot – Volume 3 (The Subliminal Verses)	$22.99
00690330	Social Distortion – Live at the Roxy	$19.95
00120004	Best of Steely Dan	$24.95
00694921	Best of Steppenwolf	$22.95
00690655	Best of Mike Stern	$19.95
00690949	Rod Stewart Guitar Anthology	$19.99
00690021	Sting – Fields of Gold	$19.95
00690597	Stone Sour	$19.95
00690689	Story of the Year – Page Avenue	$19.95
00690520	Styx Guitar Collection	$19.95
00120081	Sublime	$19.95

AUTHENTIC TRANSCRIPTIONS WITH NOTES AND TABLATURE

00690992	Sublime – Robbin' the Hood	$19.99
00690519	SUM 41 – All Killer No Filler	$19.95
00690994	Taylor Swift	$22.99
00690993	Taylor Swift – Fearless	$22.99
00691063	Taylor Swift – Speak Now	$22.99
00690767	Switchfoot – The Beautiful Letdown	$19.95
00690425	System of a Down	$19.95
00690830	System of a Down – Hypnotize	$19.95
00690799	System of a Down – Mezmerize	$19.95
00690531	System of a Down – Toxicity	$19.95
00694824	Best of James Taylor	$16.95
00694887	Best of Thin Lizzy	$19.95
00690671	Three Days Grace	$19.95
00690871	Three Days Grace – One-X	$19.95
00690737	3 Doors Down – The Better Life	$22.95
00690891	30 Seconds to Mars – A Beautiful Lie	$19.95
00690030	Toad the Wet Sprocket	$19.95
00690654	Best of Train	$19.95
00690233	The Merle Travis Collection	$19.99
00690683	Robin Trower – Bridge of Sighs	$19.95
00699191	U2 – Best of: 1980-1990	$19.95
00690732	U2 – Best of: 1990-2000	$19.95
00690894	U2 – 18 Singles	$19.95
00690775	U2 – How to Dismantle an Atomic Bomb	$22.95
00690997	U2 – No Line on the Horizon	$19.99
00690039	Steve Vai – Alien Love Secrets	$24.95
00690172	Steve Vai – Fire Garden	$24.95
00660137	Steve Vai – Passion & Warfare	$24.95
00690881	Steve Vai – Real Illusions: Reflections	$24.95
00694904	Steve Vai – Sex and Religion	$24.95
00690392	Steve Vai – The Ultra Zone	$19.95
00690024	Stevie Ray Vaughan – Couldn't Stand the Weather	$19.95
00690370	Stevie Ray Vaughan and Double Trouble – The Real Deal: Greatest Hits Volume 2	$22.95
00690116	Stevie Ray Vaughan – Guitar Collection	$24.95
00660136	Stevie Ray Vaughan – In Step	$19.95
00694879	Stevie Ray Vaughan – In the Beginning	$19.95
00660058	Stevie Ray Vaughan – Lightnin' Blues '83-'87	$24.95
00690036	Stevie Ray Vaughan – Live Alive	$24.95
00694835	Stevie Ray Vaughan – The Sky Is Crying	$22.95
00690025	Stevie Ray Vaughan – Soul to Soul	$19.95
00690015	Stevie Ray Vaughan – Texas Flood	$19.95
00690772	Velvet Revolver – Contraband	$22.95
00690132	The T-Bone Walker Collection	$19.95
00694789	Muddy Waters – Deep Blues	$24.95
00690071	Weezer (The Blue Album)	$19.95
00690516	Weezer (The Green Album)	$19.95
00690286	Weezer – Pinkerton	$19.95
00691046	Weezer – Rarities Edition	$22.99
00690447	Best of the Who	$24.95
00694970	The Who – Definitive Guitar Collection: A-E	$24.95
00694971	The Who – Definitive Guitar Collection F-Li	$24.95
00694972	The Who – Definitive Guitar Collection: Lo-R	$24.95
00694973	The Who – Definitive Guitar Collection: S-Y	$24.95
00690672	Best of Dar Williams	$19.95
00691017	Wolfmother – Cosmic Egg	$22.99
00690319	Stevie Wonder – Some of the Best	$17.95
00690596	Best of the Yardbirds	$19.95
00690844	Yellowcard – Lights and Sounds	$19.95
00690916	The Best of Dwight Yoakam	$19.95
00690904	Neil Young – Harvest	$24.99
00690905	Neil Young – Rust Never Sleeps	$19.99
00690443	Frank Zappa – Hot Rats	$19.95
00690623	Frank Zappa – Over-Nite Sensation	$22.95
00690589	ZZ Top – Guitar Anthology	$24.95
00690960	ZZ Top Guitar Classics	$19.99